READER'S DIGEST

GARDENER'S

Guide To

GROWING

ROSES

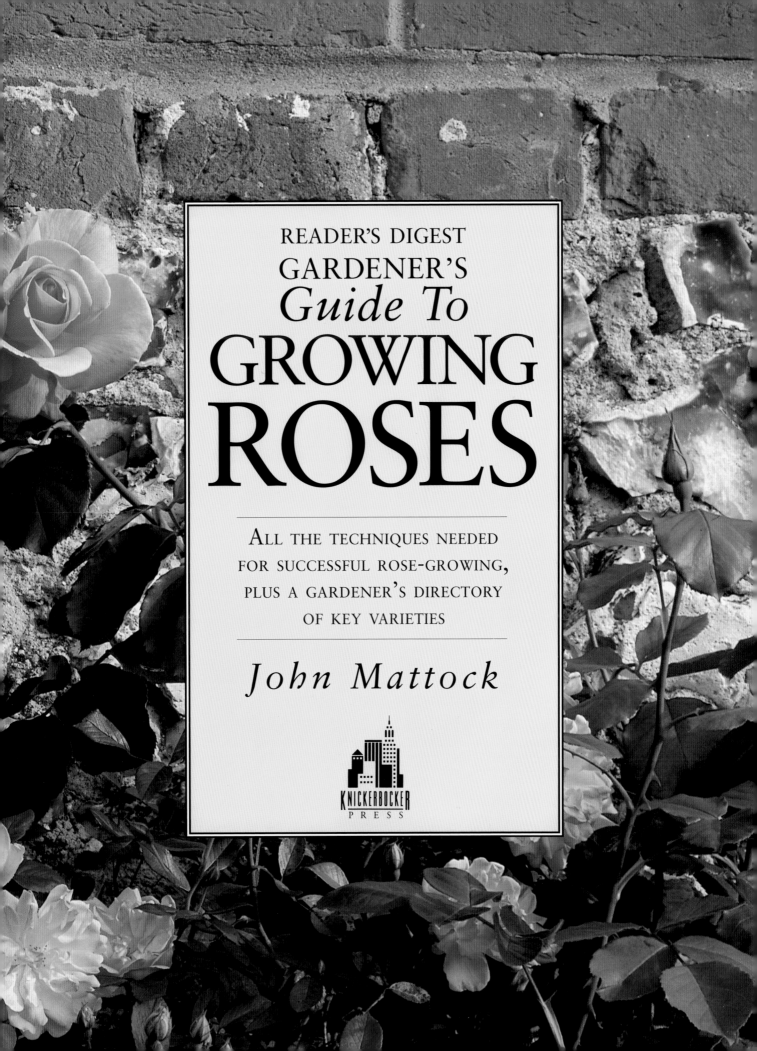

READER'S DIGEST
GARDENER'S
Guide To

GROWING
ROSES

All the techniques needed
for successful rose-growing,
plus a gardener's directory
of key varieties

John Mattock

KNICKERBOCKER
PRESS

A QUARTO BOOK

This new edition first published in 1997 by
Knickerbocker Press, 276 Fifth Avenue,
Suite 206, New York, NY 10001

ISBN 1-57715-012-0

This book was designed and produced by
Quarto Publishing plc
The Old Brewery
6 Blundell Street
London N7 9BH

Art Director: Moira Clinch
Design: Hugh Schermuly
Senior Art Editor: Antonio Toma
Copy Editors: Janet Smy and Barbara Haynes
Picture Researcher: Giulia Hetherington
Senior Editors: Sian Parkhouse and Louisa McDonnell
Editorial Director: Mark Dartford
Illustrators: Robin Griggs and Elsa Godfrey

Typeset in Great Britain by Type Technique, London W1
Manufactured in Singapore by
Bright Arts (Singapore) Pte Ltd
Printed in China by Leefung-Asco Printers Ltd

CONTENTS

INTRODUCTION

The rose has contributed much to gardens for over 2,000 years and, as a symbol of love, is familiar worldwide. It also holds a place in the development of civilization through its many uses in perfumery, herbal medicine, rituals and festivities.

Today, with increasingly low-maintenance varieties available and with the aid of modern cultivation techniques, it is possible to grow roses in most gardens in the temperate regions of the world.

However, perhaps because of its long history and many uses, the rose has inevitably inspired not only a wealth of fable and folklore, but also many false horticultural premises. How often do you hear people say: "Only clay soil will do," or "We get someone in to do the pruning – it's a mystery to us"? In the worst cases gardeners are defeated and give up: "We don't grow roses any more; they require too much attention and are always getting disease." If roses really were difficult to grow, it is unlikely they would have become so popular or so widespread. Of course it is a challenge to achieve the best results, but this applies to any gardening venture, not only to growing good roses.

This book has been written to take the mystery out of growing roses. After all, a garden should be a place of enjoyment and not a perpetual chore. It is you, the gardener, who is in charge and you must

▲ *"Summer Wine" is a vigorous modern climber which flowers throughout the summer. It is ideal for covering a high wall or fence with color.*

▶ *The modern shrub rose, "Fritz Nobis," is most adaptable. It can be grown in a border, on its own as a specimen shrub, or used to form a flowering hedge.*

never allow your garden – or your roses – to rule you. There is no sacred ritual involved in pruning, and, with the right tools, it should not be difficult.

There are also new ways of growing roses to take into account. These will give you fresh ideas, and include how to use roses in containers and raised beds and for ground cover. In addition to the exciting new varieties bred for such specific uses, the Old Garden Roses with their voluptuous flowers and fragrance still hold their own in modern gardens.

Choose your rose varieties with care, taking into account your local conditions and also the amount of spare time you have to devote to gardening. Many modern roses have been bred to thrive on the minimum amount of care, but like any other plant they will respond to occasional fertilizing. Today, there are varieties available that are more robust and healthier than ever before. Many are resistant to disease and the effects of pollution. As these trends in breeding new roses develop, there is every reason to believe that the rose will continue to flourish in the next millennium.

▲ Climbing roses are
easy to train up
almost any structure
and need little
attention, apart from
the occasional tying
in of new branches
and the removal of
dead wood.

▶ New rose plants can
be produced by the
technique of budding.
This is not difficult to
do, although a little care
and patience are needed.

I
ROSE-GROWING
TECHNIQUES

Modern cultivation techniques bring good rose growing within the grasp of every gardener.

There is no "correct" method of growing roses. It is more a matter of common sense and following the fundamental rules which govern the growing of any garden plant successfully. Because roses have been prized for so many years and are an essential part of any garden, it is inevitable that a certain amount of mystique has arisen around their cultivation. Myth and superstition are particularly prevalent with regard to planting times, pruning methods and the ways in which roses can be grown.

In spite of modern techniques some of these myths still persist and many gardeners continue to think of roses as difficult plants. Therefore, the first part of this book is devoted to reassuring you how simple it is to grow superb roses by understanding and practicing modern horticultural techniques. Older generations of gardeners may be surprised to learn that routine measures such as dead-heading and meticulous pruning, formerly governed by strict rules, have now been much simplified.

Nevertheless, certain basic principles do apply and must be observed if your roses are to flourish and flower prolifically. There is no substitute for keeping your soil fertile. Regular mulching with organic material will always pay dividends and it is essential that roses are well fed if they are to perform well. Good garden hygiene must be observed at all times. This means regular weeding and keeping your eyes open for any signs of pests or diseases so that they can be dealt with before they become established. Also pay attention to your tools. Keep them clean and sharp, especially those used for pruning.

◀ *Well-tended roses combine very well with other plants in a mixed border. Dead-heading keeps the roses flowering well.*

CLASSIFICATION

Before you decide which rose to buy, it is helpful to know the main rose groups and their characteristics.

The modern garden rose is the product of hundreds of years of selecting and breeding, culminating in the range of sophisticated blooms we now take so much for granted. It is useful to have some familiarity with the many different types of roses on offer before you plan your garden or purchase new rose plants. This will help you to choose the most appropriate type to suit your needs and also to avoid disappointment.

The World Federation of Rose Societies has redefined rose groups into 37 different divisions and sub-divisions. Although this current classification may satisfy purists, it can be bewildering to most gardeners. Fortunately, the many divisions can be simplified into just a few major groups, and it is this simplified classification that is used in this book. The basic groups described below are recognized worldwide and are compatible with those which are listed in the majority of rose catalogues.

HYBRID TEA

These roses produce large flowers singly or in small clusters from early summer to late autumn. The bushes normally grow 2–4 ft (60–120 cm) in height and should be planted approximately 2 ft (60 cm) apart. Large-flowered rose bushes combine beautifully with perennials in mixed beds and borders. Alternatively, they can be grown in beds of only roses of one color or one variety. Many varieties are grown in greenhouses to produce perfect blooms for florists.

FLORIBUNDA

Each stem carries a cluster of flowers. This results in a continuous display of color throughout the flowering season. The habit, flowering period and maintenance requirements are similar to those of the Hybrid Teas. Floribundas are chosen when the continuity of color in the garden is more important than the quality of bloom.

PATIO ROSES

Best described as short-growing Floribundas, the majority have miniaturized flowers and leaves. They flower during summer and autumn and the bushes grow to 1–2 ft (30–60 cm). Their dainty habit makes patio roses well suited to small gardens, containers and window boxes. Patio roses are also referred to as dwarf cluster-flowered bush roses and, in some countries, as "sweetheart" roses.

"Orange Sunblaze" is one of the new miniature varieties which are delightful grown in containers or window boxes, or as part of a miniature rose garden.

MINIATURE ROSES

These are tiny rose bushes growing 6–18 in (15–45 cm) high. They need the same level of cultivation and care required by other bush roses. Given this, they will flower from summer to autumn, bringing color to small beds and containers. Unfortunately they are frequently misused and planted in inappropriate places such as rock gardens or alpine situations where they do not perform well.

SPECIES

All roses originate from wild or species roses. There are between 130 and 150 species roses distributed throughout the northern hemisphere, the majority of which flower only once in the summer. Some are cultivated for characteristics other than their, usually single, flowers. For instance, some bear huge colorful hips or particularly fine foliage, and at least one species has dramatically large and translucent thorns. Many species roses make excellent garden plants for growing in borders or as specimen shrubs.

RUGOSAS

A very undemanding, hardy and disease-resistant group of roses, resulting from crosses between *Rosa rugosa* and garden varieties. The leaves are dark and prominently veined. The thorny stems will eventually form a dense thicket, making them ideal for boundary plantings. The flowers may be single or double. Most varieties have repeat flowers, sporadically, after the first flush. In some cases the flowers are followed by decorative hips.

OLD GARDEN ROSES

This group consists almost exclusively of fragrant-flowered shrub roses, now widely grown in mixed borders. They vary in habit, and also in flower size and form, which can range from single to fully double and quartered blooms. The older varieties – those introduced before 1850 – flower only in summer. Those introduced after 1850 are the immediate ancestors of the modern bush roses, and will produce their flowers recurrently throughout summer and autumn. Old Garden Roses are listed with their ancestral group names. They include the following:

Alba These are extremely hardy roses, typified by their blue-gray foliage, and pale pink, cream or white flowers.

Bourbon The first of the recurrent-flowerers, with full-petalled, rounded flowers which are heavily scented.

Centifolia Summer-flowering roses that mostly bear large, spherical, many-petalled flowers in shades of red and pink.

China Sun-loving red and pink roses, which introduced the recurrent-flowering habit to Western rose-growing.

Damask A very ancient group of mainly pink or white roses, with double, or semi-double, exquisitely perfumed flowers.

Gallica Relatively thorn-free roses in shades of rich pink, crimson or purple, sometimes splashed with white.

Hybrid Musk Repeat-flowering and bearing large blooms, these are the immediate ancestors of the Hybrid Teas.

Moss These are centifolias which have mossy growth covering the sepals and sometimes the flower stems.

Modern shrub roses, like this "Marjorie Fair," have been bred to be recurrent-flowering and fill the garden with color over a long period.

MODERN SHRUB ROSES

These can best be described as "Floribundas that are not pruned." They form bigger plants than bush roses, ranging in height from 4 to 9 ft (1.2 to 2.7 m). Most modern shrub roses produce a generous flush of blooms in mid-summer and again in autumn. They add luster to a border at a time when many other plants are not in flower.

CLIMBERS AND RAMBLERS

Before the early 19th century climbing and rambling roses were unknown in the Western world. However, after they were introduced from China, they rapidly became extremely popular. Formerly, ramblers and climbers were classified separately and the perennial question was always: "What is the difference between these two types?" In brief, a climber has a more robust stature and is capable of growing against a wall with the minimum of support. The majority of climbers arose as mutations, or sports, of Hybrid Tea varieties and consequently most climbing roses have large flowers. In contrast, a rambling rose has, by nature, very lax growth, sprawling everywhere if not supported along the length of its stems. This sprawling habit makes ramblers ideal for growing over pergolas, fences and into trees.

Traditionally both climbers and ramblers flower with a great flourish only in high summer. However, recently a breed of modern ramblers and climbers has been introduced that has the potential to flower with equal profusion in summer and again in autumn. It is now common practice to list these types of plants according to their flowering potential. Thus they appear in catalogues under summer-flowering ramblers and climbers or recurrent-flowering ramblers and climbers.

GROUND-COVER ROSES

To meet the demands of landscape architects for low-maintenance roses suitable for municipal planting, some inspired hybridizing has resulted in a range of roses with prostrate growth and a spreading habit. These are known as ground-cover roses. They vary in their spread from about 3 to 8 ft (1 to 2.5 m) and their height from as little as 1 to 4 ft (30 cm to 1.2 m). The majority are recurrent-flowering and are ideal for covering banks and slopes. Some of the more vigorous varieties make dramatic mounds of flowers and foliage, and act as very efficient weed suppressors. Before planting ground-cover roses it is imperative that the site is cleared of all perennial weeds.

STANDARD (TREE) ROSES

Strictly speaking these are not a class of rose. The description, standard, refers to the way in which they are grown. The flowering head can be formed of almost any variety of rose and is budded onto a tall stem, the rootstock. The length of the stem, measured from the ground to where the bud has been inserted, defines the type of standard and also dictates its use in the garden.

Half standards have stems of about 2 ft (60 cm) tall.

Full standards are universally grown to a height of 3–3½ ft (90–110 cm).

Shrub standards are usually budded at a height of about 3½–4 ft (1.1–1.2 m).

Weeping standards display the lax growth of some ramblers and vigorous ground-cover roses.

WHICH
VARIETIES?

Visiting rose gardens and attending flower shows will help
you to choose the perfect rose.

There are literally thousands of roses to choose from, so the task may seem somewhat daunting. However, few catalogues offer more than 300 varieties and, by convention, these are always split into their different groups. All rose growers provide details (flowering time, height, spread, etc.) about the plants they have for sale. However, some are more helpful than others – while some catalogues contain much useful information, others just give brief notes. You can also seek advice from other sources, as explained below.

VISITING GARDENS

In many countries the principal horticultural societies (see page 154) have splendid gardens which are beautifully maintained and contain plants that are well labelled. The publications of such societies, such as the American Rose Society's *American Rose Magazine*, are very informative. Many other gardens are worth visiting for the beauty of their roses but often detailed plant information is not readily available, and you will need to check with a rose retailer.

▶ *It is useful to visit gardens where roses are grown in a variety of styles. At Sissinghurst, Kent, in England the rampant rambler, "Kiftsgate," is well supported and trained into a dome shape.*

◀ *A corner of the rose garden at Mannington Hall, Norfolk, in England. Many different types of rose, including a yellow standard, make a tapestry of color.*

FLOWER SHOWS

These can be very helpful. The most important nurseries and rose breeders will be showing their best plants and newest introductions with knowledgeable sales staff usually on site. It is also interesting to visit amateur competitions but many varieties are grown specifically for exhibition and so are not necessarily good subjects for routine garden cultivation.

ROSE NURSERIES

If you have the opportunity, visit the nurseries' rose fields in the summer months. Varieties will be well labeled and usually grown in alphabetical order for easy reference. The plants you see are the rose crop that will eventually be lifted (dug up) and sold. Though they are only young, they nevertheless will give an accurate idea of their potential.

HORTICULTURAL SOCIETIES

Many societies and clubs hold lectures during the winter and organize flower shows and visits to gardens in the summer. There is also the opportunity to exchange views, solve problems and even exchange cuttings with other keen rose growers.

W HAT IS A G OOD
P LANT?

It is important to choose a well-grown, healthy rose plant.

This is easy to do when you know what points to watch for.

Rose plants from reputable suppliers should meet the criteria given here. Avoid cheap plant offers and "lost" label collections which are disappointing to grow. Most cheap plants are surplus stock from big contracts and have probably been badly stored. They are not good-quality plants.

B ARE-R OOT R OSES

Bush roses
A well-developed, moist, fibrous root system is essential, with a minimum length from the collar, or bud union, to root tip of 10 in (25 cm). There should be three healthy stems, each about 15 in (38 cm) long, growing directly from the base of the plant. Each should be at least pencil thick and show no signs of shrivelling. There must be no broken branches, and the plant should be neatly trimmed.

Climbing, rambling and shrub roses
The same as for bush roses but the stems must be a minimum of 18 in (46 cm).

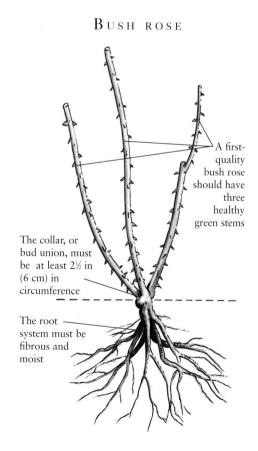

B USH ROSE

A first-quality bush rose should have three healthy green stems

The collar, or bud union, must be at least 2½ in (6 cm) in circumference

The root system must be fibrous and moist

▶ *A first-class plant, which has been well cared for, will reward the gardener with a stunning display like the mass of blooms on this climber grown against a wall.*

Patio roses, such as "Tall Story," have naturally smaller dimensions, but the root system and general appearance of the plant must still be of high quality and conform to the criteria for a healthy, well-maintained plant.

CONTAINER ROSE

The foliage must be healthy with no signs of disease

There must be no weeds or moss on the soil surface

The container must be at least 1 gallon (4.5 liters) capacity

Miniatures, patio and small ground covers

These are on a smaller scale (with stems of about 6–7 in (15–18 cm) to 18 in (46 cm), depending on the eventual height of the plant), but should still have an adequate root system.

STANDARD ROSE

Standard (tree) roses

The stems must be straight and strong with a minimum of two strong arms. It is imperative that the roots of standard roses are never allowed to dry out; the rootstock on which most standard roses are grown is particularly prone to damage when this happens.

A well-balanced standard should have three strong arms

Container-grown roses

The plants should be grown in 1 gallon (4.5 liter) pots, properly pruned and weed-free. The soil should be moist but not water-logged. The presence of lichen or moss on the soil surface indicates poor maintenance.

The perfect standard stem is strong and straight with no scars

It is very important that the roots of standards never dry out

PLANTING
NEW ROSES

*Roses will only flourish if they are planted with care
and given a good start in the garden.*

In a temperate climate roses will tolerate most sites, but there are a few in which they will not thrive. If you try to grow plants on a site from which old roses have recently been removed, growth may be poor because the soil is what is termed "rose-sick" (see page 19). Nor will roses tolerate persistent drafts, such as those that filter through gaps in hedges or around buildings, or cold winds from adjacent woodland. Do not expect roses to thrive in deep shade either, although several varieties of climbers and ramblers do reasonably well on sunless fences and walls. The soil must be well drained; roses do not like their roots to stand in water, though they will tolerate some seasonal flooding.

WHEN TO PLANT

Bare-root roses produce their best results when planted in autumn. This period can well be extended throughout the winter in mild climates, but must be completed by early spring.

Prepacked roses share the same planting times as bare-root types. Although frosty nights do not mean you have to stop planting, roses should never be handled when they are frozen.

Containerized roses give the best results when planted in late spring and early summer. Take care not to damage the root system when planting. Roses are not natural container plants and, therefore, should be transferred to their permanent homes as quickly as possible.

WHAT SORT OF SOIL?

To give new plants the maximum opportunity to establish themselves, proper preparation of a new rose bed, or the refurbishment of an old one, is vitally important.

Roses will grow in most soils, provided they are well drained. Calcareous environments (chalk and limestone, for instance) can be difficult, though not impossible, while soils high in acid (where rhododendrons and azaleas thrive) may also present problems. The acidity of the soil is measured by its pH value: neutral is 7, with acid soils being below it and alkaline soils above it. Generally roses flourish where the pH is around 6.5. Test kits to determine the pH of your soil can be obtained from most good garden centers.

The most important task before you plant roses is deep cultivation of the soil which should be done well before planting. This means double digging and adding a generous amount of organic compost – ideally well-rotted farmyard manure or garden compost – into the top layer. All perennial weeds should be removed at this stage.

On very heavy clay soils the addition of peat or a peat substitute will contribute to a more open texture and improve drainage. Clay soils do not respond well to being dug when wet and cold.

MARKING OUT

Careful marking of spacing, which should be roughly planned before ordering or purchasing plants, makes the task of planting roses much easier. A small stick placed at each position is a great help with spacing.

Bush roses are generally planted about 2 ft (60 cm) apart; climbers and ramblers about 8–10 ft (2.4–3 m) apart. Most shrub roses are more effective if planted in groups of three or five about 3 ft (1 m) apart. Standard (tree) roses, generally planted to give height to a bed or border, look ugly if planted too close together; 6 ft (1.8 m) is a suitable distance.

PLANTING MIXTURES

Whether they are bare-root or container-grown, young roses need help to enable them to establish themselves and thrive in their permanent positions. A "planting mixture" will make this much easier. The constituents are one part peat or peat substitute and one part very well-rotted garden compost (usually old leaf mold). A handful of good quality bonemeal per plant is a useful extra. Prepare this mixture before planting and make sure that there is enough for a spadeful per rose.

WHEN YOUR PLANTS ARRIVE

Modern packaging is designed to maintain the roots in a moist condition, but when bare-root plants are delivered unpack them as soon as possible. Dip the roots in water (do not soak) and if they are not going to be planted immediately heel them into a shallow trench. Large bundles of plants must be opened up or they will dry out in the middle. Should the soil be too frozen to heel them in, store in a frost-free environment, unpacked but loosely covered and away from heat. Containerized plants must be watered frequently to keep the soil moist if they are not to be planted immediately.

Siting a rose plant must be done carefully. In a mixed border, allow plenty of space around the new plant so that it gets enough light to enable it to establish quickly.

PLANTING A SINGLE BUSH

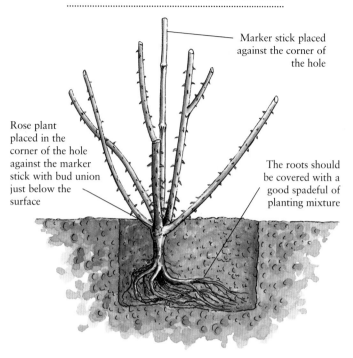

Marker stick placed against the corner of the hole

Rose plant placed in the corner of the hole against the marker stick with bud union just below the surface

The roots should be covered with a good spadeful of planting mixture

Dig a hole approximately 10 in (25 cm) square and 10 in (25 cm) deep, the corner of the hole against the marker stick. Dip the roots in a bucket of water, then place in the hole with the collar of the plant against the marker. Add a spadeful of planting mixture to cover the roots. Fill up with soil and tread down firmly.

PLANTING CLIMBERS AND RAMBLERS

Extra care is needed when planting climbers and ramblers against walls and fences because the soil here is generally of poor quality. You will need to dig a much larger hole than you would for a bush – about 2 ft (60 cm) square and 2 ft (60 cm) deep is a good working guide. Remove the old soil and add a fresh, new supply. Care must be taken to use soil that has not supported roses for at least four years. The ideal mixture consists of 60 percent heavy loam, 30 percent peat or peat substitute and 10 percent well-prepared garden compost or farmyard manure. The addition of a generous handful of good quality bonemeal per plant is also recommended. Always plant climbers at least 18 in (46 cm) away from a wall to be clear of the foundations.

PLANTING A NUMBER OF BUSHES

The secret of quick and efficient planting is good and methodical planning. A common fault, particularly when handling large numbers of bushes, is allowing the roots to dry out. Putting a damp sack over the roots will prevent this from happening.

Dig the first hole and move the soil you have removed as near as possible to the position the last bush will occupy. After placing the first bush and adding the planting mixture, dig the second hole using the soil removed here to complete the planting of the first tree. The holes are set 2 ft (60 cm) apart. This progressive system of planting means that you avoid handling the soil more than is necessary.

PLANTING A NUMBER OF BUSHES
A well-planned new rose bed with marker sticks at every planting position, set 2 ft (60 cm) apart.

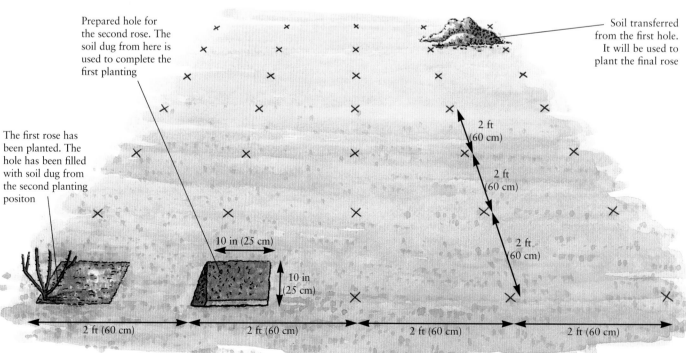

Prepared hole for the second rose. The soil dug from here is used to complete the first planting

Soil transferred from the first hole. It will be used to plant the final rose

The first rose has been planted. The hole has been filled with soil dug from the second planting positon

10 in (25 cm)

10 in (25 cm)

2 ft (60 cm)

2 ft (60 cm)

2 ft (60 cm)

2 ft (60 cm)   2 ft (60 cm)   2 ft (60 cm)   2 ft (60 cm)

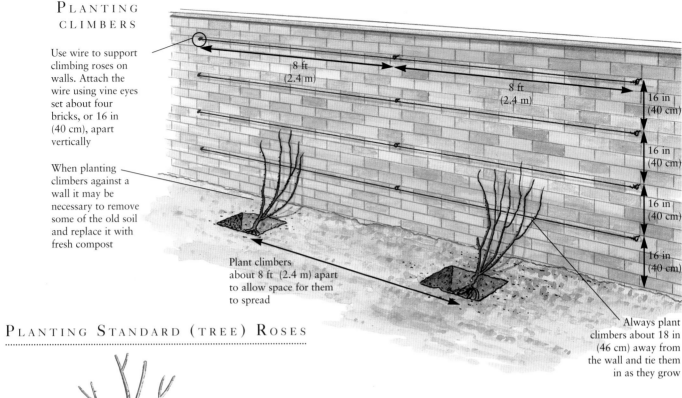

PLANTING CLIMBERS

Use wire to support climbing roses on walls. Attach the wire using vine eyes set about four bricks, or 16 in (40 cm), apart vertically

When planting climbers against a wall it may be necessary to remove some of the old soil and replace it with fresh compost

8 ft (2.4 m)

8 ft (2.4 m)

16 in (40 cm)

16 in (40 cm)

16 in (40 cm)

16 in (40 cm)

Plant climbers about 8 ft (2.4 m) apart to allow space for them to spread

Always plant climbers about 18 in (46 cm) away from the wall and tie them in as they grow

PLANTING STANDARD (TREE) ROSES

Use a good hardwood stake to support the standard. The wood should have no knots and be treated with a wood preservative

The stake must reach to just below the branches and be secured with at least two tree ties

Drive the stake well into the ground before planting the standard

A generous amount of planting mixture will help the standard to establish quickly

You need to pay great attention when planting standards. The roots must never be allowed to dry out and adequate staking is extremely important. For the stakes, select a length of high-quality lumber, without knots, roughly 2 in (5 cm) square in cross-section. It should extend from just below the standard head to at least 1 ft (30 cm) below ground level. Drive the stake into the hole before planting, and then plant against it. After applying the planting mixture, fill in the hole, firm the soil and secure with tree ties. Never use plastic string; it is abrasive and cuts into the stem.

PLANTING IN ROSE-SICK SOIL

If new roses are planted in an old rose bed they may not thrive. Rose growers say the soil is "rose-sick," a condition that causes reduced vigor in new roses planted in the bed but which does not affect the established roses there. There are several ways to overcome the problem. For small-scale planting dig a hole 1 ft (30 cm) square and as deep, remove the soil and replace with a compost similar to that used for climbers and ramblers. If the entire bed is involved, you will have to remove all the soil to a depth of 18 in (46 cm) and replace it with a fresh supply. The alternative is to clear the offending bed of the old plants and grass it over for a minimum period of four years before replanting. Sowing marigolds (*Tagetes*) and digging them in after flowering is another remedy that works well.

REPLANTING OR MOVING ROSES

Even a well-established plant can be replanted or moved successfully, provided that you do it at the right time of year. The time to choose is mid-autumn. Cut the plant down to manageable proportions – about 18 in (46 cm) for a bush, and 4 ft (1.2 m) for a climber – and remove the leaves completely. Lift the plant free of all soil and trim the root system to about 12 in (30 cm). Replant as for a bush.

PLANTING A CONTAINERIZED ROSE BUSH

Water very well before planting. Dig the hole for the bush as you would when planting a bare-root rose, but make it slightly larger. Knock the plant out of the container, taking care not to disturb the root system. Place in the hole, add plenty of planting mixture and fill in with soil. Watering must be maintained for at least six weeks (see page 24).

MAKING FEEDING SIMPLE

An easy feeding program not only improves the quality of the blooms, but also produces a healthier plant.

Roses can only grow and look their best if they are properly planted and provided with the proper nutrients at the right times of the year. Plant foods fall naturally into two groups: organic (naturally-derived) and inorganic (artificial) fertilizers.

ORGANIC PLANT FEEDS

Farmyard manure is easily available in rural areas or can be obtained at good garden centers and stores. If fresh, this manure must be stacked and allowed to mature for at least six months. Applied as a deep mulch in late winter, it will supply the basic requirements of most plants. However, never mulch with organic manure after late spring or in the autumn: in the summer it will be smelly and attract flies, while mulching in the autumn encourages new growth that could then be damaged by frosts.

Compost can be made very easily with garden rubbish, grass cuttings and degradable kitchen scraps. Turn frequently and keep the pile moist to speed decomposition. Apply in early spring, followed by a dressing of potash. Organic fertilizers are also available from garden centers.

INORGANIC PLANT FEEDS

There are fertilizers specifically produced for roses: their two main attributes are a high proportion of potash and the all-important trace elements. Although the principal ingredients of a good plant food are nitrates, phosphates and potash (represented by the letters, NPK, in manufacturers' instructions), minute quantities of trace elements (mainly iron, managanese and magnesium) should also be present. A good, high-quality rose fertilizer will contain all these ingredients. A general garden fertilizer, suitable for vegetables, can also be used.

APPLYING FERTILIZERS

Many gardeners prefer to apply organic and inorganic fertilizers in alternate seasons, thus providing a mulch that enriches the soil and a fertilizer to balance any inherent deficiences.

Always remember that roses, particularly shrub roses like the one shown here, will benefit tremendously from a boost of good rose fertilizer immediatley after the first flush of bloom.

Perishable garden rubbish (leaves, grass cuttings, weeds, etc.) and kitchen scraps can be composted to produce an excellent, organic plant food ideal for mulching around roses.

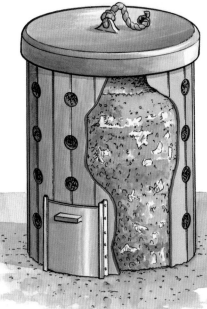

MINERAL FOODS

There are three essential foods required by plants:

Nitrates help to form good, rich green leaves and luscious growth. Because they produce rapid soft growth, they are best applied as a constituent of compound fertilizers. Cheap nitrogenous plant feeds should not be used for roses as their nitrogen content is too high.

Phosphates encourage plants to develop an adequate root system, and promote early spring growth and the general health of the plant's metabolism. They are available as bonemeal. Avoid cheap products, as these may contain acid which could burn your hands.

Potash is responsible for good hard growth, helps to create resistance to disease and produces mature wood that will withstand the rigors of hard winters.

FOLIAR FEEDS

It is possible to feed roses with a foliar feed, that is, one which is sprayed through the leaves. This is principally to correct mineral deficiencies (see page 38). However, there are general foliar feeds which will give a boost to your plants and can be applied in conjunction with aphicides and/or fungicides. Be warned: a good plant will benefit from such treatment, but it rarely helps one of poor quality.

MULCHES

Garden composts and animal manures are the most beneficial and nutritious mulches you can apply to roses. Wood chips or shredded bark have now replaced peat-based mulches. Though they have very little nutritional value, they increase water retention if applied to rose beds during the summer months. Grass cuttings can be used as a green mulch in the summer to a maximum depth of 3 in (7.5 cm). Never use lawn clippings that originate from areas where weedkillers have been used. Remember that a fertilizer must be applied *before* the summer mulch so that it is in direct contact with the soil.

▶ *Rose bed mulched with wood chips, which are very good weed-suppressors.*

◀ *Apply rose fertilizer from mid-spring to mid-summer to produce abundant flowers.*

FEEDING PROGRAMME

Late winter Apply sulphate of potash around the base of trees at the rate of 2 oz (60 g) per square yard (meter). This will help to make your plants strong and disease-resistant, and is the basis for all subsequent feeding.

Early spring Apply a heavy mulch of aged farmyard manure or garden compost. The best time to do this is immediately after any spring pruning.

Mid-spring Apply a liberal application of rose fertilizer according to the manufacturer's instructions. Usually this is a good handful per plant two or three times between spring and early summer. A dressing of dried blood in late spring will help your plants produce high-quality show blooms.

Early to mid-summer Apply the last feeding of rose fertilizer. Although a number of varieties are catalogued as recurrent-flowering, many, particularly shrub roses, need an extra boost immediately after the first flush to encourage them to produce autumn color. If roses appear to be making too much soft (unripened) autumn growth, a light dressing of potash in late summer is very helpful. Never feed roses in the autumn; they will go into the winter in an immature state and so be prone to frost damage.

WHEN AND HOW TO WATER

Established roses do not usually need watering, but in some special circumstances water must be given.

Roses are extremely tolerant plants. The very fact that they are native to temperate climates means that roses will stand a moderate depth of frost, the occasional heat wave and a reasonably generous rainfall. Because most modern roses are propagated onto a rootstock (see page 44) with a very strong root system that is capable of making 6 ft (1.8 m) of growth in a season, they will withstand considerable drought conditions.

There are certain circumstances in which watering is vital. Roses grown under glass will die unless they are watered. Not only are the plants completely dependent on irrigation, but if the supply is inadequate and the roots dry out as a result, the plant becomes prone to mildew.

In the garden, watering is vital for newly planted container-grown roses. They require regular watering for about six to eight weeks after planting out to allow enough time for their roots to become properly established. Do this by drenching the plant thoroughly twice a week with ½ gallon (2.25 liters) of water.

It is not necessary to water an established plant and doing so can even be detrimental. Freshly planted bare-root roses that have had time to settle in during the winter and spring do not require watering in the summer. Plants that have been carefully planted with a planting mixture in well-prepared soil will put up with extreme weather conditions, particularly drought, more readily. Surface watering will encourage a root system dependent on surface water and discourages the plant from growing naturally. It can lead to very soft growth (unripened wood) and the plant may not survive a hard winter.

The exceptions to the rule are newly planted rootstocks, the types of rose used for propagation. These are not normally planted until early or mid-spring and in certain circumstances do not have time to become established before a drought sets in. Heavy overhead watering (with a sprinkler) is the best method in these circumstances.

WATERING IN A GREENHOUSE

Young plants demand considerable quantities of water. A regular, thorough drenching is always preferable to a light watering. Treat in the same way as other container-grown roses (see above).

WATERING THE GARDEN

In a severe drought, watering may be inevitable but this must be done carefully. A rose plant will only benefit if it receives large quantities (several bucketsful) at intervals of ten days. Occasionally, bare-root plants, particularly climbers and ramblers, will appear to be dormant even by late spring, but a heavy watering of three to four buckets per plant will usually bring them into growth.

A bloom of the rose "Silver Jubilee" after a shower of rain. Established roses normally get all the moisture they need from the soil, but in very severe drought it may be necessary to give them water.

LIQUID FEED

There are some very sophisticated sprinkler systems through which plant nutrients can be given. These can be very efficient but must be installed by a professional.

Never water with equipment that has been used for weedkillers. It is virtually impossible to clean out cans or other utensils properly – there will always be traces of weedkiller left.

A good-quality watering can is essential. Roses in pots and window boxes require regular watering. Use rainwater if possible, and add a liquid feed to achieve flourishing plants.

WEED CONTROL

Fork over the soil and use weed-suppressing mulches to control weeds; chemical weedkillers are also effective.

Weeds are as much a problem for rose-growers as they are for all gardeners: they rob roses of nutrients and water and can stop adequate light reaching plants. They must be removed, as, if left to run wild, they will eventually take over completely.

Perennial weeds are difficult to control since they originate from rhizomes and fleshy root systems which regularly produce new growth every spring. Hardy woody plants, such as brambles, form intense thickets that can persist throughout the winter. **Annual weeds** are generated every year from seed. They can be extremely invasive but can easily be weeded out or killed with weedkillers.

IDENTIFYING WEEDS

An experienced gardener will quickly identify intrusive weeds, but if you take over a new garden, and space and

PERENNIAL WEEDS

These are the biggest nuisance and should be eliminated before planting by digging thoroughly with a fork (see page 28). Alternatively, use a total weedkiller to eradicate them completely. When they appear in established beds and borders, painting with a similar chemical will have good results.

Field bindweed
Convolvulus arvensis

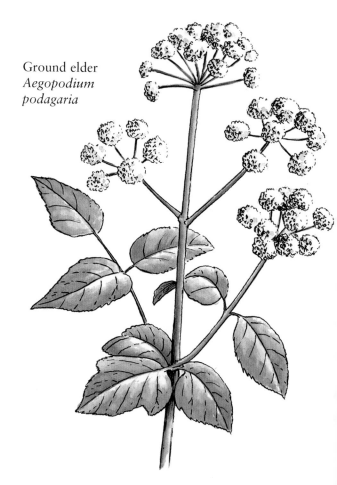

Ground elder
Aegopodium podagaria

time allow, let the garden develop naturally for a season before taking any drastic steps. Some unique horticultural gems may be revealed before a wholesale demolition of a weed habitat is undertaken. Many a long-forgotten rose has been rediscovered in this way.

CHEMICAL CONTROL

Complete eradication of weeds in a new rose bed can be achieved by the application of a *total* weedkiller. A liberal dose through a sprinkler bar attached to a watering can is the most successful method. Such weedkillers kill everything they touch – some will poison the soil thereby creating a sterile habitat that cannot be replanted for six months. Weedkiller sprays are more environmentally friendly as they are absorbed by the leaves and become ineffective when they reach the ground. However, they may kill only certain weeds, particularly perennial ones.

There are many other types of weedkiller that have proved extremely successful. The most satisfactory are so-called pre-emergent weedkillers, which create a barrier of about 1in (2.5cm) of impregnated soil which prevents the germination of annual weed seedlings. The great advantage of the pre-emergent types is that they are only active through the soil, so any drift onto the plants is of no consequence. Also, because their absorption into the soil is so shallow, they will not harm well-established plants. Those suitable for use with roses are sold under a variety of names; check the label to make sure a product is suitable for roses.

You need to clear the soil of weeds before applying the pre-emergent weedkiller. The time to do this is in late spring or early autumn and the best way of applying the weedkiller is to spray it on the rose bed using a watering can and sprinkler bar. Practice the technique first on a concrete surface just using water so that you can see how to achieve an even spray.

Weedkiller control of perennials in an established rose bed can be achieved by painting the offending intruder with a lethal dose of a total weedkiller. This has remarkable results on weeds like bindweed, perennial dandelion or couch grass. Mix the weedkiller at over half as strong again the recommended strength and apply with a paintbrush. However, take great care, as the slightest smear on your roses is fatal.

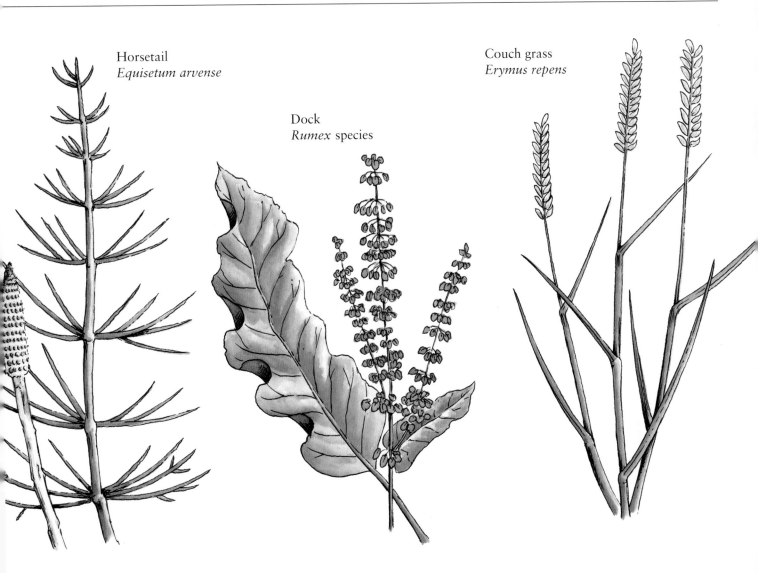

Horsetail
Equisetum arvense

Dock
Rumex species

Couch grass
Erymus repens

WEEDKILLERS

Total weedkillers
Glyphosate
Pre-emergent weedkillers
Dichlorbenil
Diquat and Paraquat

MULCHES AS WEED SUPPRESSORS

Mulches can be very helpful in helping to control weeds by suppressing their emergence. Grass clippings, shredded bark, and other organic mulches also help keep the soil moist and protected from temperature swings, and they encourage the activities of macro- and microorganisms in the soil. Some mulches, however, can increase weed problems. Manure, hay, and compost may contain viable weed seeds.

Black plastic sheeting will block weeds from spreading. Immediately after planting or in the spring, and after the application of any feed, lay black plastic over the rose bed. Disguise the plastic with a covering of bark chippings. Care must be taken to anchor the plastic securely to the ground.

REMOVING WEEDS BY HAND

If you are preparing a new rose bed, take the opportunity to fork over the soil and dispose of perennial weeds by removing their roots completely. Often this is the only time it can be done effectively. If you are dealing with an established bed, gently ease out the weeds with a fork. Care must always be taken to retread any loosened soil. Small annual seedlings can be hoed; ideally you should do this in the spring when it is dry. Only an hour or so a week is sufficient to be effective.

GROUND-COVER ROSES AS WEED CONTROL

It is possible to use ground-cover roses to suppress weeds, particularly on banks and large low-maintenance areas where wild flowers are encouraged to grow. However, all perennial weeds must be cleared first, and hoeing may be necessary until the roses are established.

PERENNIAL WEEDS *(CONTINUED)*

Perennial stinging nettle
Urtica dioica

ANNUAL WEEDS

A light hoe in the spring can usually contain these intruders; or use a pre-emergent rose-bed weedkiller.

Annual meadow grass
Poa annua

A rose which has been affected by drifting weedkiller. Although the damage looks alarming, it is rarely lethal. New growth will quickly repair the plant.

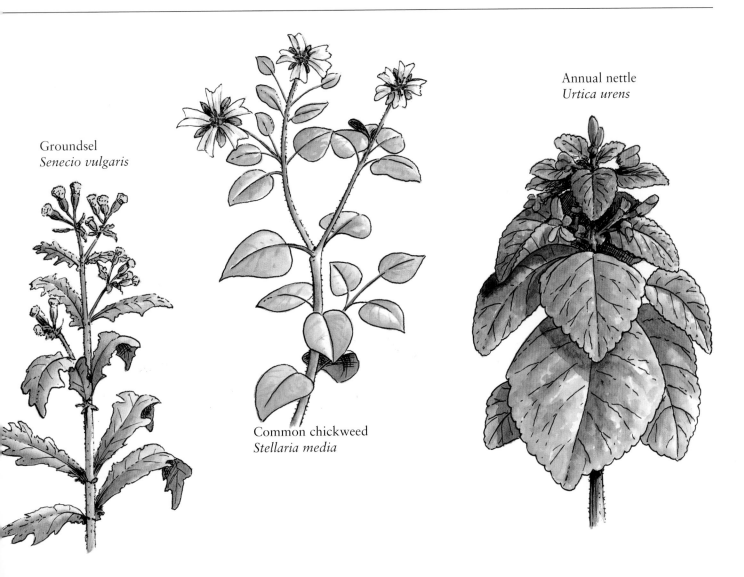

Annual nettle
Urtica urens

Groundsel
Senecio vulgaris

Common chickweed
Stellaria media

PRUNING

When pruned, roses will give
of their best.

There are no set rules governing when, where and how to prune roses. Indeed, in many places around the world where there are extremes of temperature from summer to winter, pruning is actually redundant. The persistent hard frosts of winter will reduce a plant to ground level, while in very hot climates cutting back any growth may weaken the plant.

WHY PRUNE?

All roses grown in temperate climates, and especially modern roses, need to be pruned. Left unpruned, a modern rose will grow untidily, producing an excess of wood at the expense of the flowers. As a result, the quality of the flowers will eventually decrease.

Pruning carried out during the summer months is called summer pruning, while that performed in the spring or autumn is called seasonal pruning.

NEW ROSES

New bushes for planting should be delivered in the autumn neatly trimmed down to about 15 in (38 cm). They will need cutting back in the spring by about 60 percent; patio and miniature plants should be cut back in roughly the same proportions. Shrubs, climbers, ramblers and ground-cover roses require no pruning at all in their first spring in the garden, unless they are affected by die-back (a disease which attacks young shoots and can spread to the rest of the plant). Standards should be pruned as above according to the type of rose.

ESTABLISHED PLANTS

Bush roses are pruned back by about two-thirds of the previous year's growth, one-third in autumn to prevent the bush rocking in the winter winds and another third in spring. Any dead stumps and scrubby wood should be removed at the time of spring pruning.

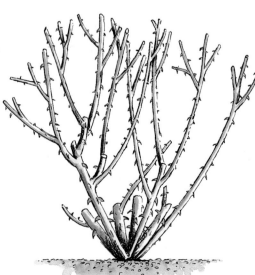

◄ *Prune established bush roses by a further third in spring. A good pair of pruning gloves and sharp hand pruners are essential.*

▶ *An established rose bush will accumulate many old stumps which must be removed.*

Miniatures and Patios Prune the same way as bush roses.

Climbing Roses Any stems that have flowered must be cut back and it is also extremely important to eliminate old and decaying wood that may harbor disease. To do this effectively, remove all the plant ties from the wall or fence and lay the plant carefully on the ground. Remove all extraneous growth and then retie the rose. If space allows, try to bend the branches slightly. This has a remarkable effect: it checks growth and encourages flowering along the stems, so avoiding bareness at the base of the plant.

▲ *An unpruned climber. The old wood makes the plant look overgrown and untidy.*

▼*A pruned climber. The old wood has been completely removed and the young wood tied in neatly. Some branches have been gently bent to encourage flowering.*

A well-tended climbing rose growing over an arch makes a striking feature.

▲ *Most of the wire supporting this rambler is old and broken, and the plant is full of dead wood which must be removed.*

▶ *The wall has now been rewired and the live wood carefully retied to give a good coverage, with as many branches as possible positioned horizontally.*

Rambling roses These produce far more flowers if old flowering shoots are shortened or removed. Therefore, treat ramblers in much the same way as climbers, removing old flowering wood.

Rambling (and climbing) roses that have been encouraged to grow into trees should be left alone. Apart from the difficulties of reaching them, they are extremely vigorous and are happier left to their own devices.

Modern shrub roses Cut back old flowering branches slightly in the spring. The aim is to give a good shape to the plant, so do not overdo this. Occasionally such roses will accumulate old worn-out branches. Remove these with long-handled loppers or a small pruning saw.

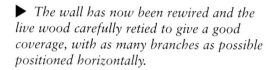

▲ *An unpruned shrub rose.*

▶ *The same rose after light pruning in the spring to cut back any old flowering branches and promote a good shape for the plant. Any old stumps should be removed with a small pruning saw.*

Rosa gallica officinalis growing in a herbaceous border. This rose will benefit from heavy dead-heading immediately after flowering, to encourage plenty of new growth for the next season's flower production.

Old Garden Roses Many of the varieties popular between the 16th and 18th centuries – the Gallicas, Damasks, Centifolias and Albas – will thrive without a great deal of attention in the modern garden. However, you can follow the practice of the old gardeners, who used to dead-head these types of rose immediately after flowering to the extent of cutting out some old wood. This is effective because most old garden roses flower on growth which is made the previous season and this is encouraged by cutting back in mid-summer.

Ground-cover roses Though these do not have to be pruned, some of the more vigorous varieties should be trimmed to prevent them from taking over the garden. The majority should not be dead-headed as they produce very pretty hips in the autumn.

SUCKERS

Sometimes a rose will produce "suckers." These are stems originating from the stock on which the rose was budded.

In time these suckers can overwhelm the plant, which will then revert to the wild rose stock. Suckers become apparent as young shoots, sometimes some distance from the plant. They usually have light green foliage with seven leaves, although this can be misleading as many new ground-cover and patio roses also have the same number.

The only safe and sure way of identifying a true sucker is to gently remove the soil and establish the origin of the growth. If it emanates from below the position on the stock where the bush was budded, then it must be a sucker. Any growth from above that position is the plant. To remove, gently pull the sucker through the ground back to the root system and pull off.

Sometimes the sucker will seem to grow from the main stem of the plant and cutting with a knife may appear to be the only way to remove it. This is not a good idea as a cut can encourage new growth. The best solution is to gouge out the sucker from the plant stem; the gouging action totally removes any traces of the sucker. Standard (tree) roses can have suckers which appear as young growths (buds) on stems; these are easily rubbed off.

PRUNING TOOLS

To achieve the best results from your

pruning, use good-quality tools.

Y ou need a sharp cutting tool in order to prune effectively, so a pair of top-quality hand pruners is essential, though expensive. The best types, which are available in a number of sizes, have razor-sharp, by-pass blades which cut side by side. The blade of another, often cheaper type cuts down onto a flat anvil and so, as this can bruise the wood, is best avoided by rose-growers. You will need a pruning saw to cut out old wood and a pair of long-handled lopping shears to reach branches that would otherwise be difficult to reach. Finally, a strong pair of leather gloves is essential: these will prevent you from being pricked by sharp thorns and help you get a firm grip on a branch.

TOOLS AND THEIR USES

All equipment used to prune roses must be extremely sharp and able to stand up to heavy use. A small carborundum stone will keep high-quality steel tools perfectly honed. Tools should be kept clean and well oiled. Every gardener should have these six essential pruning tools:

● **Stout gardening gloves** provide protection against sharp thorns.

● **Pruning saw** with folding blade for removing very thick branches and old stumps.

● High-quality **by-pass pruners** are the best to use for pruning roses.

● **Small pruners** for dead-heading and summer pruning.

● **Long-handled lopping shears** for removing inaccessible branches.

● A handy **cutting knife** is always useful.

Key

1 Stout gardening gloves

2 Pruning saw

3 By-pass pruners

4 Small pruners

5 Long-handled loppers

6 Cutting knife

DISORDERS AND DISEASES

A well-cared for rose is much better equipped to withstand the common ailments that can beset plants.

If roses are properly grown and tended, most of their problems can be overcome. A healthy, carefully selected rose plant has a great advantage over a neglected specimen struggling in an arid environment. It is not unknown for certain roses to thrive in one part of the garden, but not in another. This failure to do well is often not a symptom of some mysterious disorder, but caused by extraneous factors, such as bad drainage, drought, drafts, or even builders' rubble which has added extra calcium to the soil.

Rose leaves showing signs of manganese deficiency. This disorder is an indication of badly drained and possibly waterlogged soil. Deep cultivation can improve drainage.

A bed of roses badly affected by mildew. This gray mold is not only unsightly, but can also prevent shoots from developing properly formed flowers. However, there are some simple remedies (see page 39).

MINERAL DISORDERS

You cannot expect to grow good roses without adequate feeding and you should be aware of natural drawbacks such as inadequate soil and poor drainage. All plants must have a balanced food 'diet' which includes nitrates, phosphates and potassium (see pages 20–23). It should also contain trace elements which contribute either directly to the well-being of the plant, or as an essential catalyst (trigger), to enable the plant to absorb the food that it needs.

Look at the state of the leaves for tell-tale signs of a possible problem. Discoloration can be a sign of mineral deficiency. Most mineral disorders can be dealt with by the application of a well-balanced fertilizer with added trace elements.

Iron deficiency This can sometimes occur in limestone or chalky soils. A distinct yellowing of the leaves (chlorosis) is obvious. The remedy is to apply expensive foliar feeds known as chelates or sequestrates. Some rose varieties appear to thrive better than others in such conditions, particularly common reds and strongly-colored pinks.

Manganese deficiency Yellow bands between the veins of leaves are a sign of this condition. Treat the plants as you would in the case of iron deficiency (see left), but note that manganese deficiency is a warning that the garden is badly drained. Bad drainage can be alleviated by deep digging and adding coarse grit or sand to the soil.

Nitrogen deficiency A condition most commonly associated with poor feeding. The plant looks stunted and red spots sometimes appear on young leaves. Apply plenty of aged manure to improve the plant's appearance.

Magnesium deficiency This is relatively rare. The leaves are pale and dead areas appear in their centers as they mature. A dressing of ground limestone will solve the problem. Magnesium enables roses to absorb essential foods.

DIE-BACK

Some varieties of rose are prone to develop branches of dead or decaying wood. There are three reasons for this:

● Late in the growing season new growth fails to mature and is not ripe enough to survive the winter.
● New growth develops very early in spring and is subsequently damaged by frost. Frost-damaged wood causes whole branches to die later in the year, when the plant is producing bloom, and thus under extra stress.
● Blunt pruning equipment damages stems.

However, the treatment is simple: do not overfeed the plant, never apply any fertilizer after midsummer and give extra potash to encourage the wood to ripen fully.

Phosphate deficiency The leaves will look very pretty with blue-green and purple tints and an early leaf fall. A comprehensive fertilizer which includes trace elements is the quickest remedy.

Clear signs of die-back on a rose. This dead wood should be removed.

Potash deficiency The young leaves are reddish and develop brittle brown margins as they mature. The condition often occurs if the soil is very light (sandy); the solution is to apply a fertilizer with a high potash content in early spring. Roses are more dependent on potash than any other plant apart from tomatoes.

DISEASES

There are three principal rose diseases, all of which can be treated easily. However, as such diseases can reoccur, it is sensible to be selective and get rid of any varieties that do not grow well for you. Remember that a rose that consistently gets mildew or black spot, for instance, will pass it on both to its neighbors.

Although rose breeders have not yet developed a completely disease-resistant plant, they are now breeding roses with a good health record. However, malnutrition or bad siting will predispose plants to disease. It is always better to give roses the best chance of avoiding disease by treating them well, rather than grow them badly and then have to nurse them back to health.

Black Spot The appearance of large, clearly defined black spots on leaves followed by a rapid leaf fall are the signs of this persistent disease. Certain varieties, such as the Bourbons and roses with yellow-orange flowers, are very susceptible, but black spot is easily contained by judicious spraying with triforine. Before spraying always read the directions on the packet carefully. A balanced feeding regime is also extremely important.

Mildew A gray mold develops on the leaves and stems of young, immature growth. This is not only unsightly, it can also stop a shoot from developing mature flowers. Though there may be some relationship between a tendency to the disease and the plant's breeding, more often it is the result of cold nights, dry roots and too much nitrogen. Mildew can be controlled by fungicides; heavy watering and large doses of potash can also help.

VIRUSES

Fortunately, viruses are not very common as far as roses are concerned and rarely hinder their natural growth. The symptoms are usually light yellow veins and spots on the leaves. Faulty nursery stock is probably the biggest source of infection. If such symptoms appear, the affected plants should be cut down and the equipment used to do this sterilized with rubbing alcohol or a bleach solution after use. Most roses will then recover naturally. There is no need to destroy the plants completely.

Rust This disease used to be prevalent in many areas and was always considered fatal but, thanks to modern fungicides, it is now curable. The first signs are small, brilliant red spots, which eventually turn black, on the undersides of the leaves; the plants begin to look unhealthy and the leaves finally turn yellow. Spray as soon as the red spots appear.

PESTS

Roses, particularly modern varieties, are prey to many small predators, but control is easy with sprays.

No breeder has yet produced an aphid-resistant rose and there are other pests to contend with too. However, it is easy to combat them by spraying the affected plants. There are effective chemical treatments, but some pests will respond to to the simple remedy of spraying with cold or soapy water. Biological controls are also effective at combating most pests.

ROSE APHIDS

Rose aphids are small green or black insects which appear on young wood in spring and early summer. Commonly known as greenfly, they are particularly intrusive in early summer. They thrive on the sap of very young growth and can, in some circumstances, cause great damage by sucking the sap from the plant. Soapy water and pyrethrum are effective, as are systemic, selective aphicides. Spray at the first sign of infestation. Fly lava predators such as *Aphidoletes aphidimyza* will also help control aphid problems.

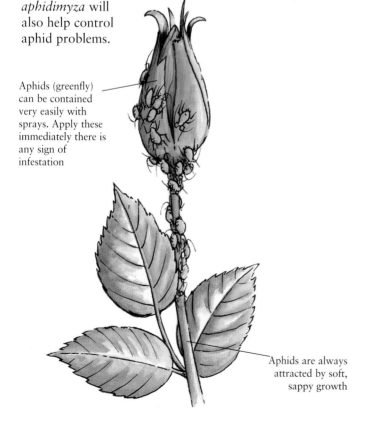

Aphids (greenfly) can be contained very easily with sprays. Apply these immediately there is any sign of infestation

Aphids are always attracted by soft, sappy growth

THRIPS

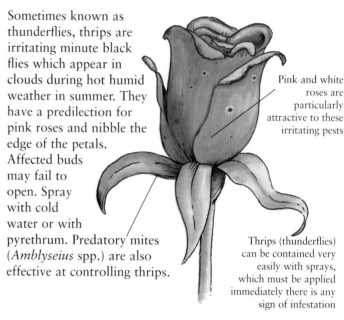

Sometimes known as thunderflies, thrips are irritating minute black flies which appear in clouds during hot humid weather in summer. They have a predilection for pink roses and nibble the edge of the petals. Affected buds may fail to open. Spray with cold water or with pyrethrum. Predatory mites (*Amblyseius* spp.) are also effective at controlling thrips.

Pink and white roses are particularly attractive to these irritating pests

Thrips (thunderflies) can be contained very easily with sprays, which must be applied immediately there is any sign of infestation

LEAF-ROLLING SAWFLY

This is a most annoying pest but fortunately it is not often encountered. The first signs of an attack appear in early summer when young, developing leaves assume a long, rolled appearance; this is caused by a chemical secreted as the leaf-rolling sawfly deposits its eggs. To prevent a reoccurrence, spray the soil underneath the affected plant with Fenitrothion late during the following spring – this will kill the fly when it emerges from the ground before it can deposit its eggs on the plant. The light-colored fly is rarely seen; the damage it causes is far more obvious.

Typical damage – unsightly but of no long-term consequence. Sometimes a caterpillar can be found within the leaf roll; it should be destroyed

Damage caused by the leaf-cutting wasp is unsightly, but relatively harmless.

CATERPILLARS, BEETLES AND LEAF-CUTTING WASPS

The majority of these are almost impossible to control. Beetles are the only ones that are easily visible and most pundits recommend removing them by hand. When spraying for aphids check that the aphicide you are using will also combat caterpillars and leaf-cutting wasps. Control Japanese beetles by monitoring rose bushes and taking immediate action before infestation is severe. Hold a jar half-filled with ammonia beneath Japanese beetles and tap them into the jar, where they will swiftly die.

OTHER PROBLEMS

Roses can be affected by weedkiller drifting onto them, and young foliage appears contorted as a result. Do not remove the affected leaves, as the plant will grow out of this irritating intrusion. Leaves also become malformed if plants are watered using equipment that has has not been washed out properly after previously containing weedkiller.

Balling is when the outer petals rot and the bloom fails to open; this usually happens in persistent wet weather

Balling is common in some of the older Hybrid Teas which have a very high petal count

A typical young bloom which has failed to develop due to a combination of wet weather and probably mildew.

Balling of young flower buds Occasionally, particularly in persistent wet weather in summer, rose blooms rot on the plant before developing. This condition is known as balling and is almost impossible to control. What you can do is increase your application of potash to produce a hardier plant. Another similar problem is the development of a weak neck with the flower rotting off as a result. This is treated in the same way and can also be controlled with a mildew spray. The two conditions are most often seen in older varieties of large-flowered (Hybrid Tea) roses.

Frost damage Some plants appear to survive a particularly hard winter only to collapse when in full growth during the following growing season. This is because the tissue damage caused by severe winter weather only becomes apparent when great demands are made on the plant. To avoid this, take the precaution of applying a dressing of potash in the early autumn, which will encourage hardiness. Late frost in the spring can "scorch" young growth. No treatment is required in this instance as nature will heal the wounds and produce new growth rapidly.

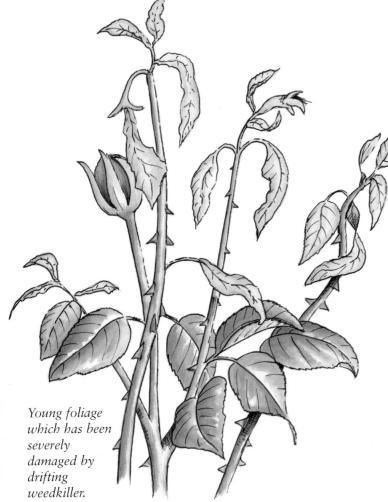

Young foliage which has been severely damaged by drifting weedkiller.

CLIMATIC HAZARDS

Roses are resilient plants and, if well-fed and protected,

able to withstand severe winter weather.

The rose is naturally tough and very hard to kill. In extremely hot, dry conditions it will probably lose its leaves but, once the wet season arrives, it will regenerate. Generally speaking, the hotter the climate, the less likely a plant is to respond to cutting back.

Roses do best in cold winters if their new growth has ripened and hardened before cold weather arrives. Avoid fertilizing after mid-summer, though you can provide an extra dose in autumn. The most cold-hardy roses are *R. blanda*, *R. canina*, *R. rugosa*, and *R. virginiana*, which withstand temperatures as low as –35°F (37°C), Albas, Damasks, and Gallicas are hardy to –22°F (–30°C). Hybrid Teas, Grandifloras, and Floribundas can tolerate –20°F (29°C) if the crown is protected by a mound of soil. Centifolias, *R. californica*, and *R. wichuraiana* may survive temperatures as low as –10°F (–23°C).

Much rose damage is caused by winter drainage problems. A badly drained garden where the roots are subject to frequent freezing is bound to lead to problems. To help prevent these, cut down bush roses by a third in the autumn (see page 30); this will stop them rocking in the wind and so loosening the soil around the roots, which can be damaged when the soil is frozen. The greatest protection any plant can receive is a deep covering of snow every winter.

◀ *Protecting a rose will reduce the damage caused by desiccation, the drying up of a frozen plant in cold, sunny conditions.*

PHYSICAL PROTECTION

The simplest way of protecting your plants against severe winter weather is to envelop them completely with chips or chopped straw held with sacking or plastic. However, the most effective method is to cut the plants down to about 18 in (45 cm) and then surround them individually with a wire or plastic cage with a circumference of about 3 ft (1 m). Fill this with bark or straw in late autumn and remove it in early spring. Alternatively, you can fill large buckets or pots with straw and place them upside-down over the cut-down plants. Place a heavy weight on top to stabilize them, if necessary. Standard (tree) roses can be protected by bending them over and covering. To do this, remove the soil completely from one side of the plant and slightly loosen it on the other. Apply gentle pressure at the uncovered base of the plant until it is lying flat on the ground. Cover with straw.

MICROCLIMATES

There is a very narrow dividing line in some areas between mild and harsh climates. For example, some gardens in California are almost tropical, while others in the same state are desertlike and still others are alpine. Obviously height above sea level is a determining factor, but shelter in the lee of a mountain range can also be helpful (in some areas this also affects the rainfall). Within the garden itself there can also be microclimates, which you will discover through experience – for example, house and building walls can cause drafty corners or provide extra warmth and shelter depending on where plants are sited.

◀ *A walled garden with its own warm microclimate and plenty of light encourages early growth and exuberant flowering.*

▲ *Modern roses have the potential to flower well into the autumn. Once they have been damaged by frost, cut the plant down by a third to reduce rocking in winter winds.*

PROPAGATING

With a little care, amateur rose growers can propagate their own roses or even breed entirely new varieties.

As an alternative to spending money on a new rose plant, propagate one yourself. There are two simple methods you can use: vegetatively or from seed. Neither is very complicated, although care, patience and a certain degree of perseverance are needed.

VEGETATIVE PROPAGATION

It is virtually impossible to sow the seeds of your favorite rose and grow an identical plant. This is because all modern roses are cross-bred and their seeds produce an extraordinary mixture of leaf and color. To breed true you must propagate with part of the chosen variety itself.

BUDDING

In the course of their breeding the majority of modern roses have lost the ability to produce a satisfactory root system which gives a good plant and high-quality blooms. Almost all rose plants that are for sale are grown on a special rootstock. To get your roses to grow like this, you need to utilize a process called budding.

Budding is the introduction of a leaf bud from another plant into the rootstock. If a stem is cut from stock plants and trimmed for the purpose of budding it is called a stick of buds. Standard (tree) roses are budded into the barrel of the stem according to the height required.

The essential tool for budding is a budding knife. This is usually made from surgical steel with a single blade and a handle with a flat chiselled point which helps to open up a T-shaped incision on the stock. Good quality raffia is needed to tie the buds onto the rootstocks.

Wild (species) roses grow very vigorously. The rootstocks of certain wild roses are therefore ideal for propagating new roses.

ROOTSTOCK

In the past, ordinary dog rose (*Rosa canina*) rootstock was used for budding. However, it proved very unreliable in certain soils, and so today more sophisticated stocks are used, either *R. laxa* or *R. inermis*. These are raised from seed in their millions by specialist growers. They can be purchased from nurseries and are usually available from early winter to early spring. Plant out, leaving about 7 in (18 cm) between plants. In dry springs they may need watering. They are usually ready for budding by early or mid-summer.

The tremendous range of color available in modern roses is a testament to the skills of rose hybridists around the world.

H O W T O B U D

Make a T-shaped cut on the stem with your budding knife and open the bark to reveal the cambium. This is the growing part of the stock which is in effect the sap source; if this is not present the stock is dry and budding cannot take place.

Slice off a single bud, including a portion of the bark, the leaf stock and a sliver of wood underneath the bud. Remove the sliver, trim the bark and insert into the stock. Wind raffia around the bud and tie to secure. A successful budding will heal immediately and the raffia will rot away.

The budded stock will generally remain dormant until the following spring when you should neatly remove the top half of the stock with pruners. This is called heading back. As the season progresses the dormant bud will begin to grow and by mid-summer will have developed into a substantial plant. By autumn the plant will have matured and be ready to be transferred to its permanent position.

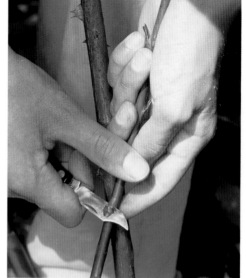

A skilled propagator uses a very sharp budding knife to take the bud from a stick of buds, ensuring that as thin a sliver of bark as possible is removed. It is advisable to use a budding knife as seen below in stage 2.

1 A stem prepared to receive a bud. A T-shaped cut has been made and the bark peeled back to reveal the cambium.

3 This is the detached bud.

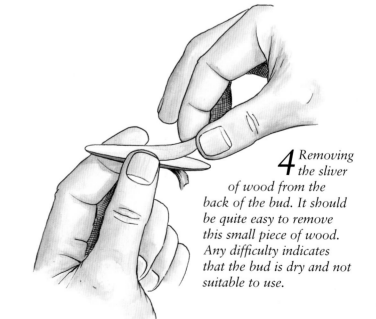

2 Removing the bud from a stick of buds. Use an extremely sharp budding knife to cut a sliver of bark with a bud, the leaf stock and a small piece of the stem.

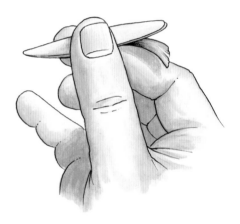

4 Removing the sliver of wood from the back of the bud. It should be quite easy to remove this small piece of wood. Any difficulty indicates that the bud is dry and not suitable to use.

5 *A trimmed bud, ready for insertion into the stock. Do not handle the bud more than is necessary. It is a good idea to practice on some surplus wood before doing the real thing.*

6 *Inserting the bud into the stock. The stock should have been cut open just before you position the bud and should be completely free of dirt.*

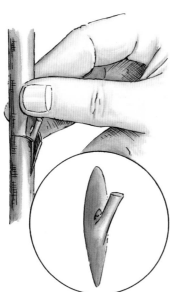

7 *Securing the bud. Tie the bud with a strand of raffia wrapped tightly and neatly round the stem. The raffia will rot away naturally in the autumn.*

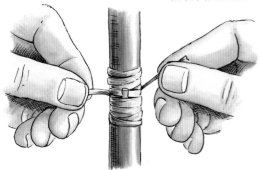

8 *Heading back. After the bud has taken (been accepted by the stock), it will remain dormant until the following spring. Head back the bud in spring by cutting off the stock just above the bud.*

9 *The growing bud. As the sap starts to rise, the bud will grow quite quickly, until, in mid-summer, the plant will have developed enough to produce flowers.*

GRAFTING

This is, in principle, the same as budding, the difference being that the whole stem is used. The technique is most commonly used to propagate roses grown primarily for cutting and some miniature rose varieties.

Grafting is usually carried out in the spring. The grafted plant is grown on in a greenhouse to produce results very quickly.

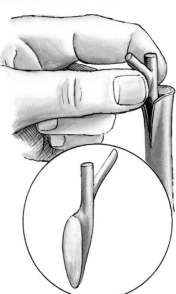

CUTTINGS

Many other types of plant are propagated by cuttings and it has now become a popular technique for some ground-cover, patio and miniature roses. In late summer or early autumn cut a piece of stem up to about 9 in (23 cm) in length, with about four or five leaves, from the stock plant. Remove all except the top two leaf shoots but keep the buds. Cut the base of the stem through the lowest bud. Dip the cutting into water, then in hormone rooting powder, and plant in a trench to which some sharp sand has been added. After filling in and firming about 1¼–2 in (3–5 cm) of the cutting is left above ground level.

In a normal season the cutting will have grown a good root system after 12 months and be ready for placing in its permanent position. This process can be accelerated by taking cuttings later in the season (early spring), bringing them into a greenhouse in pots and using gentle bottom heat. Good plants can be grown very quickly in this way but for some reason they rarely have enough ripened wood to be planted out until the following spring.

1 Choosing a cutting. In early autumn select a healthy, well-ripened stem. It should have good, disease-free leaves too, if possible. Remove the stem from the main plant. Remove all except the two top leaves.

2 Trimming the cutting. Remove the soft growing tip or old bloom, leaving about 9 in (23 cm) of wood. Pull off all but the top two leaves and cut the base of the cutting through a bud and slightly gouge out.

3 Planting a cutting. Prepare a shallow trench and add some sharp sand to it Dip the end of the cutting in water and dust with hormone rooting powder. Plant firmly in the trench, leaving the leaves visible.

GROWING ROSES FROM SEED

To produce a completely new rose of your own making is probably the most exciting part of rose growing. It is quite a chancy business, but this absorbing process is not beyond an amateur gardener's capability, despite demanding time and attention to detail. Although there are only about twenty professional rose hybridists around the world, there are many amateur hybridists who have succeeded in producing varieties which have since become world famous.

The majority of roses produce hips containing seeds, which, when germinated, do not breed true. The seeds of species roses are the exception.

A well-grown group of colorful roses in The Royal Horticultural Society's garden at Wisley, Surrey, England. Rose breeders carefully choose the parent plants of hybrid roses like the ones shown here.

continuously all summer. Similarly, if you think your favorite pink rose could be improved by a better shape to the bloom, look for one with the perfect form. Choose your ideal parents and pot them on in early autumn. A large pot is required for each plant: approximately 5 gallons (22.5 liters) is about right. Leave the plants outside to become established, bringing them into the greenhouse in mid-winter. Immediately cut back by half. Provided the greenhouse is frost-proof no heating is required. The plants will grow naturally and be in bud by the middle of the spring.

The basic requirements for hybridizing are few, but a greenhouse is necessary as it is virtually impossible to do in the open air. It is also vital to understand the anatomy of a rose bloom and to know which are the reproductive parts of the plant.

The *sepals* are the leafy outside protective covering of the young blooms. The *petals*, in many respects the most important part of any rose, play no part in the breeding process. As the petals develop the male *stamens* with their *pollen*-bearing *anthers* become apparent; the grains of pollen are very fine, almost like flour. In the center of the bloom is the *stigma* which leads to the *ovary*, the female part of the flower. The fertilization of the bloom is completed when the pollen, applied to the stigma, is absorbed by the *styles* and fertilizes the ovary, which eventually develops into the seed head (hip).

PARTS OF THE FLOWER

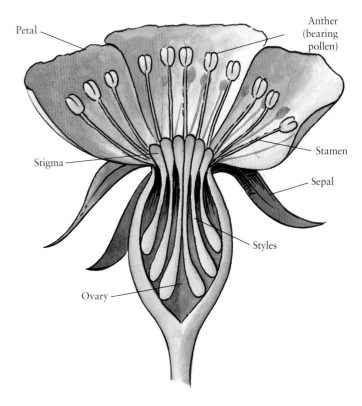

Petal

Anther (bearing pollen)

Stigma

Stamen

Sepal

Styles

Ovary

HYBRIDIZING

To breed roses in a more controlled way, it is necessary to hybridize, or fertilize the flowers of the rose by hand. Successful rose breeding must be systematic, and this includes several tasks: making a very careful selection of breeding varieties; fertilizing the flowers; raising the subsequent seedlings; and selecting those that will be potential new varieties.

The first decision is which roses you choose as the parent plants. If you are fond of a lovely red rose in the garden but would like to breed a greater continuity in its flowering, then you could cross it with one that flowers

HOW TO HYBRIDIZE

As the plants develop and come into bud, the operative part of breeding begins. Allow the flower heads of the mother plant to develop until the sepals are completely reflexed and the first petals are showing color. Gently tear off the petals to reveal the immature stamens. Remove the anthers from the stamens, thus preventing self-pollination; this process is called emasculation.

Allow the male parent to develop normally. When you can see the pollen on the anthers, collect it in a small dish and keep it dry. Once the stigma on the emasculated flower becomes sticky, usually about 24 hours after the petals are removed, it is ready to receive the pollen which will have ripened and become light and floury. Load the pollen onto a small camelhair brush and gently brush the surface of the stigma. If you are pollinating several distinct varieties, you should sterilize the brush after each pollination by dipping it into surgical spirit. Allow it to dry before using again.

Eventually the pollen is absorbed by the stigma and travels down to the ovary where fertilization occurs. If successful the seed head (hip) will develop and ripen by late autumn. Water the plants sparingly and keep the atmosphere dry. It is useful to attach small tags to each plant giving details of the parentage.

2 Emasculation The flower head after the anthers have been removed to prevent self-pollination. The rose is now in a receptive condition to receive the pollen.

3 Applying the pollen with a camelhair brush. About 24 hours after the anthers have been removed the stigma ripens and becomes receptive to pollen.

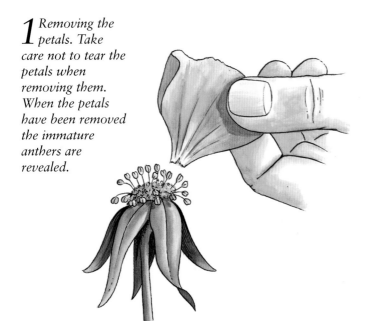

1 Removing the petals. Take care not to tear the petals when removing them. When the petals have been removed the immature anthers are revealed.

4 Plant labelled after pollination. It is useful to label the plant with a record of the pollen donor.

Given good growing conditions and plenty of sun the plants will flower (with very small blooms) and the hips will be ready to harvest in the late autumn. Some of the hips will turn yellow and even red. Rose seeds are notoriously difficult to germinate, but, to accelerate the process, take the seeds out of the hips and place them in small pots of seed compost with some vermiculite. Keep moist.

Store the pots for about two months in a warm environment away from mice. In early spring, subject them to a moderate degree of cold, 25°F (–4°C), for about ten days by putting them in a refridgerator. This process is called stratification. In a greenhouse with a minimum temperature of 45°F (7°C), sow the seeds in seed compost at a depth of about ½in (1.5cm). If the seeds are planted in early spring germination can occur within two weeks, but more often it is after six to eight weeks. The rather thin-looking plants will flower eight weeks later at a height of about 10in (25cm). Although you can see quite quickly what the flowers of the new crosses are like it is not possible to judge the quality of the whole plant at this stage.

The range of color produced by cross-breeding can be a revelation. Once the plants have become established (after about 12 months), the skill is to select the best candidates to grow on. Growing on is achieved by taking budwood from the seedlings and budding onto rose stocks grown outside (see page 46). After two or three years you can assess the subsequent progeny.

WHAT'S IN A NAME?

Roses often used to be named after famous historical characters, such as Cardinal de Richelieu, or mysterious ladies such as Louise Odier and Baronne Prévost. In recent years there have been some less romantic names because sponsorship and a handsome fee can be attracted by naming a rose after a commercial product: "Glenfiddich," "Whisky Mac," "Benson and Hedges Gold," "International Herald Tribune" and many others have been introduced in this way. Some roses are named and sold in order to raise funds for a particular charity, for example, "The Valois Rose" (The Royal Ballet School) and "Queen Mother" (Royal United Kingdom Benificent Association). Other names have universal appeal, such as "Congratulations," "Silver Jubilee" or "Loving Memory," even though they are not associated with any person or product. It is possible to call a new rose by whatever name you please, but of course, if it is to be sold commercially, it must be a name that is not in current use for another rose.

S E A S O N A L
M A I N T E N A N C E

Follow a simple seasonal maintenance routine for

healthy, well-tended roses.

Roses are not difficult plants and most will grow, and even flower after a fashion, with almost no special treatment at all. However, by establishing a simple maintenance routine, you can maximize their full potential and fill the garden with color and scent from early summer until the first frosts. Caring for them properly is not a time-consuming business: just two or three hours a week spent on simple tasks, enjoyable in themselves, will make an enormous difference to the appearance and performance of your roses. However, it is vital to know precisely at what time during the year specific maintenance should be carried out. By following the program on the next three pages you will ensure that you are feeding, dead-heading, etc., in the appropriate season. Neglected roses will not give of their best, and yet it is so simple to care for them efficiently. By maintaining your roses well you will achieve greater disease resistance and in return they will give a wonderful display of blooms during the flowering season.

A regular light hoeing will eliminate weed seedlings. It also works in any fertilizer that has been applied and creates a layer of fine dust which helps to contain moisture.

WINTER, EARLY SPRING

Not a very busy season for the gardener, so this is the time to make some routine checks.

- Check tools and do any necessary maintenance or replacing. Assess stocks of fertilizers and pesticides and, if necessary, re-order.
- Inspect supports and ties for standard (tree) roses and replace if necessary.
- Tie in any wayward climber and rambler shoots.
- Give a dressing of sulphate of potash, 2 oz (60 g) per square yard or meter, particularly to plants that were disease-prone last year.
- Rose plants in a greenhouse should all have been pruned by now and a minimum temperature of 40°F (5°C) established.

EARLY, MID-SPRING

Probably the busiest time in the garden.

- Prune bush and patio roses.
- Apply pre-emergent weedkillers.
- Paint any perennial weeds with a very strong weedkiller.
- Apply a good mulch of well-rotted organic manure.
- In mid-spring give all roses a liberal application of a good rose fertilizer.
- Head back stocks that were budded last summer.
- Plant fresh stocks for budding in the coming season.
- Raise minimum temperature in the greenhouse to 50°F (10°C), but give plenty of ventilation on sunny days.

In winter the minimum temperature in the greenhouse should be 40°F (5°C). Good hygiene is essential; clean the glass before winter sets in.

Sharpen tools ready for pruning. It is vital that roses are pruned with sharp implements. Prunings must be collected immediately and cleared away for burning later.

Roses will thrive after a good mulch of well-rotted manure after pruning in the early spring.

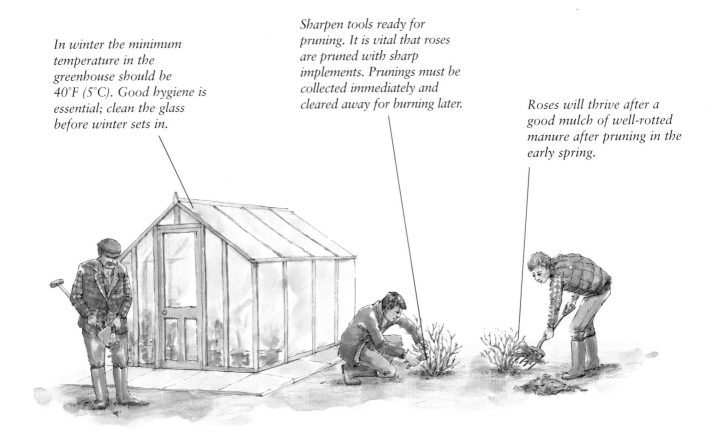

LATE SPRING, EARLY SUMMER

The rose garden is now beginning to show color with the species first to flower.

- As a result of late frosts some young shoots will appear blind. Cut these back by half to encourage new growth.
- Spray with a systemic aphicide against aphids.
- If you are hybridising, your pollination program should now be in full swing.
- Remove suckers.
- Mulch with lawn-mowings, but make sure they are no more than 3 in (7.5 cm) deep and free of weedkiller.
- If you are growing roses specially for exhibitions and want them to produce large blooms, give them a feed of dried blood.

MID-SUMMER, LATE SUMMER

The most rewarding season to enjoy the rose garden.

- Check for any hint of fungus disease and deal with it immediately with a good spraying. Use a mixture of aphicides and fungicides, ideally with added foliar feed.
- Give the final application of fertilizer after the first flush of flowers.
- Dead-head old garden roses; while doing so cut out any old wood.
- Dead-head bush and any recurrent-flowering shrubs, unless, of course, the rose is being grown for its hips.
- Finish budding.
- Make the most of any opportunities to visit gardens and flower shows.
- Order new roses in good time for planting them out in the autumn.

Trace the origins of suckers back to below the point of propagation on the plant.

Remove any stems that have not survived the winter – they are a potential source of disease and decay.

It is important to spray both the top surfaces and the undersides of leaves.

Apply fertilizer close to the rose, but never allow any to go on the plant itself.

Early Autumn, Late Autumn

The time to review the performance of your plants and replace any that are unsatisfactory.

- Take cuttings of any patio, miniature, and ground-cover roses for which you would like more plants.
- Prepare beds for new roses.
- If the soil is too wet when new plants arrive, unpack them and heel them in.
- Plant new roses.
- In late autumn prune and tidy up ramblers and climbers. Tie in any loose shoots.
- Cut back established bush roses by a third to reduce the risk of wind damage.

Early and Mid-Winter

The dormant season for roses.

- Continue planting new roses for as long as the weather remains mild.
- Check and, if necessary, re-stake and tie standard (tree) roses.
- Check the ties of all ramblers and climbers – they should be thoroughly secured.
- In very cold areas protect plants from frost damage.
- If you want to reposition established plants, this is the time to do it. Dig them up carefully, and then trim the roots and cut back the top growth by two-thirds before replanting in the new position.
- Check for signs of predator damage and, if necessary, repair rabbit-proof fences.

Tie in all loose shoots on climbers to prevent winter gale damage.

Always plant a standard with the supporting stake reaching to just below the head.

Cut down bushes by a third immediately after the first frosts.

Protect plants from frost damage by surrounding them with straw or wood shavings.

SHOWING ROSES

Enthusiastic rose growers will want to show their prize blooms,
not just to family and friends, but at public rose shows.

Showing the results of your gardening efforts to your friends and relations is very satisfying and can be a source of great pleasure. Participating in competitions is a further step in this natural enjoyment. Indeed, the majority of the principal horticultural societies around the world originated from such friendly rivalry. Many of the popular large-flowered (Hybrid Tea) bush roses and cluster-flowered (Floribunda) bush roses are fine for the show bench, although the purist exhibitor tends to grow what are called "exhibition" varieties. Note, though, that these are often poor garden plants.

GROWING ROSES FOR EXHIBITION

The largest blooms are achieved by good feeding and specific pruning. An additional feed of dried blood at 2 oz (60 g) per square yard or meter in the late spring or early summer helps flowers to reach maximum size. As far as pruning is concerned, generally it is advisable to cut down the plants somewhat harder than you would do normally. As they begin to shoot, allow only the strongest growth to develop, cutting or rubbing off all the weaker stems so that the plant's energy is concentrated.

◀ *Roses are shown well at the annual Chelsea Flower Show. This exhibit was staged by the Royal National Rose Society and displays some selected modern varieties.*

▶ *Another Chelsea exhibit of roses grown to perfection.*

▶ *Disbudding a Hybrid Tea. Remove lateral (side) buds at an early stage.*

CUTTING AND CONDITIONING

Roses for showing should be cut with as long a stem as possible, up to 18 in (45 cm). Cut them 48 hours in advance, in order to give them a good drink before transporting them. Place them in deep buckets of water to which a conditioning preservative has been added and keep them in the dark. This treatment helps blooms keep their size and color and gives them a longer vase life.

TRANSPORTING

Rose blooms can be transported for considerable distances fairly easily. They can either travel wet, standing in deep buckets of conditioned water, or dry in flat florists' boxes. Whichever method is used, they must be packed tight to allow no freedom of movement. Always pack in ordinary newspaper, never in tissue paper, which will stick. As blooms will start to open in transit, some of the large ones may need to have a thick wool strand tied loosely around them to stop them developing too quickly.

DISBUDDING

Large-flowered (Hybrid Tea) bush roses As the flowering stem develops, some varieties will produce multiple heads. These side shoots must be removed as they appear, to encourage the plant to grow larger single blooms.

Cluster-flowered (Floribunda) bush roses Although these varieties naturally grow in clusters they have an annoying habit of producing a leading bloom well ahead of the rest. Remove this at an early stage of development in order to produce a more evenly distributed spray.

▶ *Adjustable bloom protectors will give a purity of petal color and reduce weather damage.*

COVERING

Most shows forbid the exhibiting of rose blooms that have been covered, for instance, under glass. However, protection from the elements in the final stages of development of the flower is quite admissible and small cones can be bought for this purpose. The skill comes in selecting the correct blooms for this extra attention.

◀ *Disbudding a Floribunda. Improve the appearance of Floribundas by removing the central bud. By doing this you will achieve the maximum number of flowers.*

The huge range
of Old Garden
Roses available
in mid-summer
allows flower
arrangers to be
very competitive
in decorative
classes at flower
shows.

▲ *Cottonwool plugs are used to hold the petals of this show bloom in position until judging starts. They must be removed before the judges assess the rose.*

◄ *Producing a "box of six" demands large blooms of flawless quality and excellent presentation.*

► *A pretty vase of modern varieties, attractively arranged with some species rosehips.*

STAGING AND DRESSING

On arrival at the show it is important that the blooms be unpacked immediately and allowed to acclimatize in the warm atmosphere of the tent or hall. The first thing to do is to confirm the time of judging.

Blooms can be manipulated, that is, dressed, to enhance their appearance. Although rose petals reflex (curve back) quite naturally they will usually require some persuasion to be at their best at the time of judging. This can be done by gently brushing them with a dry camelhair brush, but any sign of damage, such as small tear marks, is quickly spotted by the judges and is called over-dressing. Any ties must be removed. Finally, labelling, whether mandatory or optional, will always impress the judges if it is clear and accurate.

TYPES OF STAGING

Horticultural competitions are organized into classes, and for roses there are innumerable variations based on three distinct styles:

Vases Usually the show schedule will stipulate the number of blooms or stems, varying from a single bloom to nine or twelve. In some shows the vase is provided by the organizers.

Boxes Individual blooms are exhibited in a very precise manner in custom-made boxes. Although sometimes considered a relic of the past, they are still popular and great emphasis is placed on bloom size and perfection.

Bowls The most decorative form of competition. The emphasis here is two-fold, the quality of bloom and the arrangement of color. The size of the bowl is usually specified, as is the number of stems. Sometimes the bowls are provided.

WHAT JUDGES LOOK FOR

The first thing a judge does is to count the number of entries, and confirm that each entry matches the standard required. That generally means counting the stems, confirming the size of the container and, in some instances, the size of the exhibit. Many shows now demand that *all* varieties are labeled. There is nothing more disheartening than to see the letters N.A.S. (not according to schedule) on the judges' card.

If the display meets the regulation requirements, the judge will then look for blooms that are fresh, showing no signs of manipulation, not over-dressed, well presented and true to variety and type.

▲ *All types of rose were originally descended from the species, or wild roses, like this Rosa hugonis.*

▼ *In this garden roses fill a flowerbed, backed by a wall, on which a climbing rose flourishes.*

▶ *There are so many ways in which to use roses. Here, the modern shrub rose, "The Fairy," makes a pretty container-grown standard.*

II
ROSE DIRECTORY

Roses are remarkably versatile with varieties to suit every situation.

Roses flourish in gardens throughout the temperate regions of the world. They come in many shapes and sizes: from vigorous ramblers and sprawling shrubs to neat patio roses and tiny miniatures. These very different types of roses can be used in various ways, and the Rose Directory is filled with good ideas to show you how they can play a vital part in your garden, whether its size is large or small.

As a source of cut flowers and fragrance, roses are unsurpassed, but their delicate beauty belies the fact that many are tough and undemanding, capable of forming impenetrable hedges or low cover for steep banks and awkward corners. Climbers and ramblers can be trained to climb through trees or over arches and pergolas, in addition to adorning walls or masking unsightly fences. Many Old Garden Roses have fine foliage as well as exquisite and often wonderfully scented flowers which mingle beautifully with other plants. On a more intimate scale, miniature and patio roses can be used in raised beds and containers. Some of the new and exceptionally healthy ground-cover roses give a marvellous display when grown in this way.

Roses are traditionally associated with formal gardens, and standard roses, in particular, play an important part. They act not only as a centerpiece for a rose bed, but also as eye-catching specimens in their own right. For those who enjoy their roses massed in beds, there is an enormous range of Hybrid Teas and Floribundas to choose from. Even in wild and woodland gardens roses have a place, filled by the wild or species roses which have appealing flowers and are often adorned with lustrous hips in autumn.

In each section an illustrated selection of outstanding, reliable and currently available roses is set out for your reference. Use this guide to bring increased beauty, scent and style to your garden.

HOW TO USE THE ROSE DIRECTORY

There are outstanding roses for every situation in the garden:

the directory will help you make the perfect choice.

In the following directory, roses of different types are grouped according to their use in the garden. The varieties and species have been carefully selected from the hundreds of roses available as the very best for a particular purpose or to suit a particular situation. In this way the gardener is assured of success, and saved the time of searching through catalogues and the disappointment of costly mistakes. The roses in any one section may cross the bounds of classification and have been chosen to include the assortment of colors, shades, and degrees of fragrance. The sections are as follows:

Colorful Hedges (pages 66–69)
Ideas on how to divide your garden into separate "rooms" using modern shrub roses, Hybrid Musks, and the outstanding "English" roses.

Rose Boundaries, (pages 70–73)
Surround your garden with a beautiful and impenetrable barrier of the best Rugosa roses. Tolerant of clipping, these have fine flowers, foliage, and hips.

Climbers on Walls and Around Doors (pages 74–77)
Provide a country-cottage welcome by training climbing roses around your door and over the garden wall to give a wonderful display of color.

Climbing Through Trees (pages 78–81)
Make more of a mature tree by allowing a rambling or climbing rose to festoon its branches with summer flowers.

Arches and Pergolas (pages 82–85)
Frame your garden with an arch of climbing roses, or enjoy the shade beneath a rambling rose-covered pergola.

Pillars and Tripods (pages 86–89)
An elegant way of adding height to your border is to train a climbing rose up a stylish vertical support.

Containerised Beauty (pages 90–93)
An exquisite selection of patio and modern shrub roses capable of flourishing in a pot or tub of generous proportions.

Making a Miniature Rose Garden (pages 94–97)
Inspiring ideas on how to display miniatures, the daintiest of the roses.

Patio Roses (pages 98–103)
Patio roses, with their long flowering season and wide range of colors, are the perfect choice for planting around your outdoor entertaining area.

Roses in Beds (pages 104–111)
A selection of the best Hybrid Tea roses for block planting in smart, geometric shapes.

Roses in Borders (pages 112–119)
Old Garden Roses, with their voluptuous blooms and fragrance, are the epitome of an English flower garden.

The Formal Rose Garden (pages 120–125)
Generous clusters of flowers and neat growth make Floribundas ideally suited to formal designs.

In Splendid Isolation (pages 126–129)
Some outstanding modern bush and shrub roses which have the stature to make a specimen plant and a dignified focal point for any garden.

A Carpet of Roses (pages 130–133)
Tough, easy to care for and free-flowering, ground-cover roses can be used to fill many an awkward corner or slope.

Raised Beds and Rock Gardens (pages 134–137)
Several ground-cover roses are particularly dainty and possess the neat but spreading form appropriate for these special situations.

Happy Marriages (pages 138–141)
Enchanting ideas for combining roses with all sorts of other plants to bring greater variety and interest to your garden.

Roses as Cut Flowers (pages 142–145)
Perfect flower form and long stems make a good rose for cutting. These attributes are found among the Hybrid Teas, Bourbons and some Floribundas.

Standard (Tree) Roses (pages 146–147)
A versatile way of growing roses on stems of varying height. The grafted variety determines the shape, which can range from a miniature tree to a majestic weeping standard.

The Wild Rose Garden (pages 148–149)
Roses as nature intended: the charm and undemanding nature of the species roses are admirably suited to an informal style of gardening.

ROSE DIRECTORY KEY

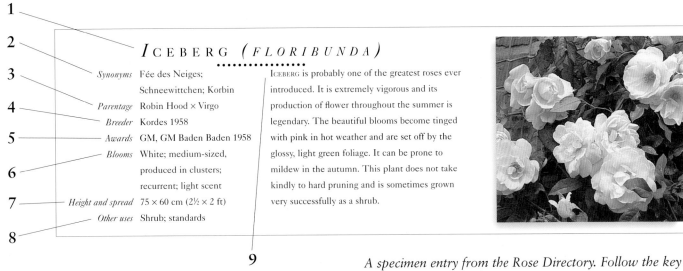

1

2

3

4

5

6

7

8

ICEBERG (*FLORIBUNDA*)

Synonyms Fée des Neiges; Schneewittchen; Korbin

Parentage Robin Hood × Virgo

Breeder Kordes 1958

Awards GM, GM Baden Baden 1958

Blooms White; medium-sized, produced in clusters; recurrent; light scent

Height and spread 75 × 60 cm (2½ × 2 ft)

Other uses Shrub; standards

ICEBERG is probably one of the greatest roses ever introduced. It is extremely vigorous and its production of flower throughout the summer is legendary. The beautiful blooms become tinged with pink in hot weather and are set off by the glossy, light green foliage. It can be prone to mildew in the autumn. This plant does not take kindly to hard pruning and is sometimes grown very successfully as a shrub.

9

A specimen entry from the Rose Directory. Follow the key for an explanation of each heading.

1 *Name* The correct name of the rose is followed by its classification.

2 *Synonym(s)* These are given only where applicable, with the popular, or common, name always appearing first. This is followed by other names the rose has been listed under. If the variety has been introduced within the past 25–30 years its international registered name will be the first of the synonyms.

3 *Parentage/Origin* The parentage is supplied by the breeder, who always quotes the female parent first. The term "seedling" indicates that a parent is used only as breeding material by the hybridizer, and is not a recognized variety. In the case of Old Garden Roses and species roses this information is not appropriate and the place of origin of the roses is given together with its date of introduction into cultivation in the West.

4 *Breeder* The name of the breeder is followed by the earliest known date of introduction into cultivation.

5 *Award(s)* These are given only where applicable. Internationally recognized bodies award medals and certificates to worthy roses after trial at their show grounds or gardens.

6 *Blooms* The blooms are described in terms of color; size, whether they are single or double, borne singly or in clusters; whether they flower recurrently or once only in summer; and whether they are scented or not.

7 *Height and spread* The approximate dimensions of the rose are given. Inevitably these will vary according to the soil and situation in which the rose grows, and on how it is pruned and cultivated. As a rough guide, a bush rose should attain these dimensions after about three years and a climber or rambler after about five or six.

8 *Other uses* Although a rose is primarily suited to the section in which it falls, it may be suitable for other sections or for exhibiting.

9 *Description* The appearance of the roses is described with details of habit, foliage and other attributes, including hips, autumn color and disease-resistance, as well as any special pruning or feeding requirements.

ROSE AWARDS

UK
Royal National Rose Society (RNRS) awards are always given first. They are abbreviated as follows:

PIT President's International Trophy for the best new rose (RNRS)
GM Gold Medal (RNRS)
CM Certificate of Merit (RNRS)
TGC Trial Ground Certificate (RNRS)
EM Edland Medal for Fragrance (RNRS)
JM James Mason Memorial Gold Medal (RNRS)
ROTY Rose of the Year (nominated by the British Rose Industry, British-bred roses only)
BARB British Association Representing Breeders

International
AARS All American Rose Society
Other awards are given by rose organizations based in, for example, Belfast, Dublin, Geneva, Madrid, New Zealand, Paris, Portland, USA, Rome, The Hague.

COLORFUL HEDGES

Roses look very effective grown as ornamental,

flowering hedges within the garden.

Many of the larger varieties of rose have found a niche in the garden as very good hedging plants. They have many practical advantages, but their greatest contribution is color and scent; they are also excellent for dividing different areas of the garden.

The Hybrid Musks, originally developed at the beginning of this century, are enjoying a revival as excellent plants for imaginative landscaping. As hedges they provide color and scent over a long period. Like all good roses they profit from well-prepared, clean soil to which plenty of organic manure or compost has been added. Bare-root plants, the cheapest type, must be planted by the end of the winter. Spaced about 3 ft (1 m) apart they will probably be slow to start but in about three years should mature into a magnificent thick hedge.

A hedge of one variety can be slightly overpowering in a small garden, but a mixture of three or four varieties, of similar habit, produces a memorable display. Careful dead-heading encourages a well-balanced plant. Many Hybrid Musks produce a great flush of color in early to mid-summer and then take a rest. Longer flowering can be encouraged by removing old blooms, but even more effective is a generous dose of good rose fertilizer well before the first flush is over.

Ornamental hedges can be planted using a wide range of cultivars and species, but you should always consider the suitability of a variety for the particular location. A wide range of roses, some mentioned in this section, can help to fulfil these requirements. *Rosa mundi*, a striped Gallica, is perfect as a frame for herbaceous plants; its flowering period is short but compensated for by the profusion of flowers. Some of the very bushy floribundas, such as "Korresia" and "The Times Rose" (see pages 120–125), will give color and prettily divide areas in the vegetable garden. The two patio roses "Sweet Magic" and "Gentle Touch" (see page 91) are possibly the most original hedging plants. Planted about 18 in (46 cm) apart they will produce a low, dense hedge.

The criteria for this type of mixed planting are ease of maintenance and compatability. When grown to form an ornamental hedge, many roses respond well to almost casual trimming in season.

A rose hedge in full flower symbolizes high summer, and is an excellent frame for many garden plants. This mixed Rosa mundi *and* R. gallica officinalis *hedge is a perfect example.*

C O N S T A N C E   S P R Y   (M O D E R N   S H R U B)

Parentage Belle Isis × Dainty Maid
Breeder Austin 1961
Blooms Bright pink; large, double,
cupped, produced in clusters;
summer-flowering; strong,
Old Garden Rose perfume
Height and spread 5 × 5 ft (1.5 × 1.5 m)
Other uses Climber on rich soils

CONSTANCE SPRY was the first and probably the most successful seedling from David Austin. It has an arching habit and plenty of large deep green leaves.

B U F F   B E A U T Y   (H Y B R I D   M U S K)

Parentage William Allen Richardson ×
seedling
Breeder Bentall 1939
Blooms Apricot to buff, fading to pale
primrose; double, produced
in clusters; recurrent; strong
scent
Height and spread 5 × 5 ft (1.5 × 1.5 m)
Other uses Shrub; cut flowers

BUFF BEAUTY, once it achieves full size, makes a handsome contribution to the garden. It has an awkward habit when young, later developing arching, spreading branches which need careful dead-heading to encourage a good shape. Its dark green leaves are subject to mildew.

F E L I C I A   (H Y B R I D   M U S K)

Parentage Trier × Ophelia
Breeder Pemberton 1928
Award CM 1926
Blooms Light pink shaded with
salmon; double, produced in
clusters; recurrent; scent
Height and spread 5 × 5 ft (1.5 × 1.5 m)
Other uses Borders; bush

FELICIA is one of the freest-flowering shrub roses ever bred. The sprays of bloom appear almost continuously but must be sustained with heavy feeding and seasonal dead-heading. It has a spreading habit with dark green medium-sized leaves.

G O L D E N   W I N G S   (M O D E R N   S H R U B)

Parentage Soeur Thérèse × (*Rosa
pimpinellifolia* × Orminston
Gold)
Breeder Shepherd 1956
Blooms Light golden yellow; large,
single, produced in small
clusters; recurrent;
moderately sweet scent
Height and spread 5 × 5 ft (1.5 × 1.5 m)
Other uses Borders; bush

GOLDEN WINGS is a very popular, attractive plant with large, prominent single blooms which require regular dead-heading to encourage continuous flowering. This rose is probably the closest that you can get to the perfect shrub. It is bushy with light green leaves and resists disease well.

GRAHAM THOMAS (MODERN SHRUB)

Parentage Charles Austin × (Iceberg × seedling)
Breeder Austin 1983
Blooms Deep rich yellow; medium-sized, double, slightly cupped; recurrent; scent
Height and spread 5 × 5 ft (1.5 × 1.5 m)
Other uses Semi-climber; cut flowers

GRAHAM THOMAS is a useful shrub that is probably the finest in its color range, and is a fitting tribute to a world-renowned plantsman. It has an upright, arching habit and large dark green leaves.

MARJORIE FAIR (MODERN SHRUB)

Synonyms Red Ballerina; Red Yesterday
Parentage Ballerina × Baby Faurax
Breeder Harkness 1978
Award TGC 1976
Blooms Carmine with a white eye; small, single, produced in large clusters; recurrent; little scent
Height and spread 4 × 4 ft (1.2 × 1.2 m)
Other uses Borders; bush

MARJORIE FAIR, as one of its synonyms suggests, is a red version of Ballerina, with large mopheads of extremely prolific flowers. This plant is bushy in growth with small glossy leaves and needs regular dead-heading but only light pruning.

PENELOPE (HYBRID MUSK)

Parentage Ophelia × seedling
Breeder Pemberton 1924
Award GM 1925
Blooms Creamy pink; semi-double, produced in large clusters; recurrent; strong scent
Height and spread 5 × 5 ft (1.5 × 1.5 m)
Other uses Borders; bush

PENELOPE is considered the finest rose in this range. The clusters of creamy pink flowers have an elegance to them which is enhanced by a pleasing scent. Feed this rose well, particularly in mid-summer, to encourage autumn flowers. It has a spreading habit and deep green, bronze-tinted leaves.

YESTERDAY (MODERN SHRUB)

Synonym Tapis D'Orient
Parentage (Phyllis Bide × Shepherd's Delight) × Ballerina
Breeder Harkness 1974
Award CM 1972
Blooms Rose pink to lilac pink; small, semi-double, produced in clusters; recurrent; strong scent
Height and spread 3½ × 3½ ft (1.1 × 1.1 m)
Other uses Borders; bush

YESTERDAY's almost light purple clusters of flower are quite astonishing in their profusion and make it a very useful plant which adds an extra dimension of color in the garden. It is low-growing with small, shiny leaves.

OCTAVIA HILL (MODERN SHRUB)

Synonym	Harzeal
Parentage	Seedling × seedling
Breeder	Harkness 1995
Blooms	Clear pink; large, very double; recurrent; strong scent
Height and spread	4 × 4 ft (1.2 × 1.2 m)
Other uses	Borders; bush

OCTAVIA HILL, when lightly pruned, will develop into a large bush rose reminiscent of the new "English Roses," but far superior. It is robust and very bushy with large deep green leaves.

MOONLIGHT (HYBRID MUSK)

Parentage	Trier × Sulphurea
Breeder	Pemberton 1913
Award	GM 1913
Blooms	Lemony white; semi-double, small- to medium-sized, produced in sprays; recurrent; good scent
Height and spread	4 × 4 ft (1.2 × 1.2 m)
Other uses	Borders; shrub

MOONLIGHT is a typical Hybrid Musk and one of the earliest to be introduced from this line of breeding. It is a large shrubby plant with small- to medium-sized leaves.

MARY ROSE (SHRUB)

Synonyms	Ausmary; Country Marylou; Marie Rose
Parentage	Seedling × The Friar
Breeder	Austin 1983
Blooms	Deep rose pink; large, double; recurrent; good scent
Height and spread	4 × 3 ft (1.2 × 1 m)
Other uses	Borders; cut flowers

MARY ROSE is an interesting, free-flowering "English Rose" which has a good length of stem and is very useful for flower arrangements. It has slightly uneven shrubby growth and medium-green foliage.

L.D. BRAITHWAITE (SHRUB)

Synonym	Auscrim
Parentage	The Squire × Mary Rose
Breeder	Austin 1988
Blooms	Bright clear crimson; large, double, with incurved petals; recurrent; scent
Height and spread	3 × 4 ft (1 × 1.2 m)
Other uses	Borders

L.D. BRAITHWAITE was the first bright red rose in the innovative breeding line "English Roses" pioneered by David Austin. This variety was achieved by crossing the Old Garden Roses with modern hybrids. It is a very bushy plant with grayish-green foliage.

ROSE BOUNDARIES

Rugosa roses make wonderful, thick flowering hedges which need little maintenance.

By far the best choice for a hedge boundary between the garden and the outside world are roses from the Rugosa group. These plants were discovered in Japan and China but adapted so well to so many regions of the Western world that they are mistakenly considered indigenous in Scandinavia and North America. Although the genus *Rosa* is not generally considered evergreen, the Rugosas retain their leaves well into the winter. Their growth is generally dense and forms a decorative, impenetrable hedge – the perfect intruder-proof barrier.

Rugosa roses are recognizable by their thick, deeply ribbed, leathery leaves, stems which are covered in small, very fine thorns, and an almost total resistance to disease. The large pink, red or white, mostly single, heavily scented flowers are recurrent flowering, and most varieties produce a bumper harvest of large red hips in the autumn which are a great attraction to birds. Maintenance is very simple: Rugosas do not like being pruned, so they should be allowed to grow naturally; most varieties will quickly mature into well-proportioned plants.

To achieve a thick boundary hedge, set the plants about 2–3 ft (60–90 cm) apart; they should establish themselves quickly, reaching a height of about 5–6 ft (1.5–1.8 m). If the plants become straggly, they can be reduced once every six years in late winter to about 1–2 ft (30–60 cm). A rejuvenated plant will quickly appear the following season.

Spectacular hedges can also be created using vigorous ramblers and climbers which will eventually form dense thickets. Rustic woodwork and trellis frames can be used to form the hedge, but these structures are difficult to maintain and seasonal weatherproofing requires the temporary removal of the plant material. The easiest way to construct dramatic border hedges is to grow the roses against simple wire fencing. This gives initial support to vigorous plants and keeps them off the ground. They will grow freely and completely hide the wire.

◀ *"Schneezwerg" has an extremely long flowering season and therefore makes an excellent decorative hedge. By the end of the summer there will be both hips and flowers.*

▶ *Rugosa roses like "Pink Grootendorst" have very sharp thorns. These act as powerful deterrents to any would-be intruders and Rugosas are therefore ideal for impenetrable boundary hedges.*

FRAU DAGMAR HARTOPP (RUGOSA)

Synonym	Frau Dagmar Hastrup
Breeder	Hastrup 1914
Blooms	Silvery pink; medium, single, produced in small clusters; recurrent; scent
Height and spread	4 × 3 ft (1.2 × 1 m)
Other uses	Borders; bush

FRAU DAGMAR HARTOPP is considered by many to be the prettiest of the Rugosas. The beautiful blooms are produced continuously, complemented by a rich harvest of large spherical hips. It makes a very good low-growing, bushy hedge with dark green foliage.

ROBUSTA (RUGOSA)

Synonyms	Korgosa; Kordes Robusta
Parentage	R. rugosa × seedling
Breeder	Kordes 1979
Award	CM 1980
Blooms	Deep wine red; large, single, produced in small clusters; recurrent; scent
Height and spread	5 × 4 ft (1.5 × 1.2 m)
Other uses	Semi-climber; bush

ROBUSTA has a strong, upright habit and dark green leathery leaves which make it very suitable for hedges. A thick hedge of this variety has been described as impossible to penetrate.

PINK GROOTENDORST (RUGOSA)

Parentage	Sport of F. J. Grootendorst
Breeder	Grootendorst 1923
Blooms	Soft pink; double, produced in clusters, with frilled petals resembling *Dianthus* (pinks); recurrent; very little scent
Height and spread	5 × 3 ft (1.5 × 1 m)
Other uses	Borders; bush; cut flowers

PINK GROOTENDORST is a fascinating plant, having a myriad of small flowers on long stems. The original to which it sometimes reverts, F. J. Grootendorst, is dull red with nothing like the same appeal. It grows vigorously, and is upright in habit, with prominent, very sharp thorns and dull green leaves.

ROSERAIE DE L'HÄY (RUGOSA)

Parentage	Sport of unknown Rugosa seedling
Breeder	Cochet-Cochet 1901
Blooms	Rich wine red; large, double and flat; recurrent; strong scent
Height and spread	6 × 5 ft (1.8 × 1.5 m)
Other uses	Borders; bush

ROSERIE DE L'HÄY, a hardy Rugosa, is blessed with very heavily scented blooms but, unusually, no hips. The red, almost purple, blooms are produced continuously. It has vigorous dense growth and dark green leathery leaves with pleasing autumnal yellow tints.

RUGOSA ALBA (*RUGOSA*)

Origin	Introduced *circa* 1870
Blooms	Pure white; large, single, produced in small clusters; recurrent; strong scent
Height and spread	5 × 5 ft (1.5 × 1.5 m)
Other uses	Bush

RUGOSA ALBA is a spectacular plant which produces enormous orange-red hips which look very dramatic against the dense foliage. It has a bushy, compact way of growing, and large, leathery wrinkled leaves which turn gold in autumn. When grown as a specimen bush it should be pruned lightly.

RUGOSA RUBRA (*RUGOSA*)

Synonym	R. rugosa atropurpurea
Origin	Introduced before 1867
Blooms	Wine red; large, single; recurrent; good scent
Height and spread	5 × 5 ft (1.5 × 1.5 m)
Other uses	Bush

RUGOSA RUBRA and *Rugosa alba* are both very attractive plants and share an almost identical habit which produces very solid hedges. The very large hips are a great attraction to birds in the autumn.

SCHNEEZWERG (*RUGOSA*)

Synonym	Snow Dwarf
Parentage	Rugosa seedling
Breeder	Lambert 1912
Blooms	White; small, semi-double, produced in clusters; recurrent; scent
Height and spread	6 × 3 ft (1.8 × 1 m)
Other uses	Borders; bush

SCHNEEZWERG has an extremely long flowering season that results in myriads of small bright red oval hips forming alongside autumn flowers. It has a vigorous upright growth with small, light green leaves. When planted closely it can be clipped to make a strong natural barrier.

BLANC DOUBLE DE COUBERT (*RUGOSA*)

Parentage	Rosa rugosa × Sombreuil
Breeder	Cochet-Cochet 1892
Blooms	Pure white; large, semi-double, produced in small clusters; recurrent; strong scent
Height and spread	6 x 5 ft (1.8 x 1.5 m)
Other uses	Borders; bush

BLANC DOUBLE DE COUBERT is a magnificent plant of tremendous vigor, but it is apt to grow leggy. It has strong, dark green leathery leaves. The hips are not as plentiful as those on some of the other Rugosas, but this lack is more than compensated for by the splendid scent.

CLIMBERS ON WALLS AND AROUND DOORS

*A climbing rose grown on a wall will give a
stunning display of color.*

No other plants can provide such a feast of color on walls as roses. Over a century ago climbing roses were mainly summer-flowering, but in the last 30 to 40 years breeders have created plants which will clothe walls with color for most of the summer, and many will produce a good show on a north aspect. Varieties, additional to those mentioned in this section, which will grow in less than ideal conditions are: "New Dawn" (see page 84) and "Aloha," "Dortmund," and "Golden Showers" (see pages 87-89).

When choosing roses for walls and around doors, general guidelines to remember are that yellow looks particularly good against stonework; some reds are completely lost on red bricks; pinks may not look good against modern paintwork and thorny varieties should not be planted close to well-trodden pathways.

For a climbing rose to grow successfully against a wall it should have a robust stem so that the amount of tying that is required can be reduced. Plants with a rambling habit and lax growth will demand a lot of attention and tying in.

The best support for climbing roses is wires strung horizontally with the aid of vine eyes. Wires can be removed very easily, when necessary, with a pair of pliers and restringing can be done quickly and simply. It is not advisable to grow climbers against trelliswork on a wall: they can grow behind the trellis, and if maintenance needs to be carried out on the wall, the whole framework may have to be demolished.

The average climbing rose will fill a space about 8–10 ft (2.4–3 m) wide and should be planted 18 in (45 cm) away from the base of the wall. To give the plants a good start the soil must be well prepared before planting (see page 18). Roses newly planted against walls may be slow to establish, but if adequate compost has been used copious watering will speed up growth.

Climbers and ramblers should be pruned in late autumn. Pruning them then makes it easy to identify old and decaying wood and means that all the shoots can be firmly secured before the winter storms. Use soft string rather than plastic ties which can be very abrasive.

The climbing rose "Parade," with its profusion of flower from early summer until late autumn, is ideal for growing against a wall. It will do well on a north- or east-facing wall.

SYMPATHIE (CLIMBER)

Parentage William Hansman × Don Juan
Breeder Kordes 1964
Blooms Rich blood red; medium-large, produced in small clusters; recurrent; light scent
Height and spread 10 × 10 ft (3 × 3 m)
Other uses Pillars; cut flowers

SYMPATHIE is the best rose in its color range; it is robust with deep green foliage; very free-flowering and tolerant of most positions.

COMPASSION (CLIMBER)

Synonym Belle de Londres
Parentage White Cockade × Prima Ballerina
Breeder Harkness 1973
Awards TGC 1972; EM 1973; GM Geneva
Blooms Pink, shaded apricot; large double, produced in clusters; recurrent; very good scent
Height and spread 10 × 10 ft (3 × 3 m)
Other uses Fences; pergolas

COMPASSION is one of the finest climbers. The vigorous profusion of quality blooms recurring throughout the summer and autumn is enhanced by a wonderful scent and magnificent, healthy, deep green foliage.

SCHOOLGIRL (CLIMBER)

Parentage Coral Dawn × Belle Blonde
Breeder McGredy 1964
Blooms Rich coppery orange; perfect double; recurrent; very good scent
Height and spread 12 × 8 ft (3.7 × 2.4 m)
Other uses Pillars

SCHOOLGIRL is a very popular plant, largely because of its big, fragrant blooms. It grows fast and has large, glossy, dark green leaves. Careful training will prevent it becoming leggy. The scent is ample compensation for any extra trouble taken.

PINK PERPÉTUÉ (CLIMBER)

Parentage Danse du Feu × New Dawn
Breeder Gregory 1965
Awards CM 1965
Blooms Deep pink with carmine reverse; medium, double, produced in clusters; recurrent; moderate scent
Height and spread 10 × 8 ft (3 × 2.4 m)
Other uses Pillars

PINK PERPÉTUÉ's large clusters of blooms and big, dark green leaves give this plant an attractive appearance. Growth is slow and it requires plenty of feeding and regular dead-heading. Rust can be a problem.

MERMAID (*CLIMBER*)

Parentage   R. bracteata × tea rose seedling
Breeder   Paul 1918
Awards   GM 1918
Blooms   Primrose yellow; large, single with prominent amber stamens produced in small clusters; recurrent; moderate scent
Height and spread   15 × 15 ft (4.6 × 4.6 m)
Other uses   As a sprawling shrub

MERMAID is a classical rose with superb simple flowers which are produced in profusion. It will grow in sunless locations but can be damaged by hard winters. It has stiff, vigorous growth and glossy green foliage. Young growth is very brittle and needs careful tying in.

MAIGOLD (*CLIMBER*)

Parentage   Poulsen's Pink × Fruhlingstag
Breeder   Kordes 1953
Awards   TGC 1953
Blooms   Bronze yellow, large, semi-double, produced in small clusters; summer-flowering; very good scent
Height and spread   8 × 8 ft (2.4 × 2.4 m)
Other uses   Pillars; vigorous shrub

MAIGOLD is one of the earliest roses to flower and will sometimes bloom again in the autumn. It has a strong sweetbriar scent. Growth is vigorous with large, dark green leathery leaves and very thorny stems

ZÉPHIRINE DROUHIN (*CLIMBER*)

Synonym   Charles Bonnett
Parentage   Not applicable
Breeder   Bizot 1868
Blooms   Cerise pink; medium, semi-double, produced in clusters; recurrent; very good scent
Height and spread   10 × 6 ft (3 × 1.8 m)
Other uses   Pillars; prune to grow as a shrub

ZÉPHIRINE DROUHIN is a widely grown climber, famous for its thornless stems, but prone to mildew. However, the scent more than compensates for the care needed to control the mildew. Growth is moderate with dull green foliage and thornless stems. There is a thornless pale pink cousin, Kathleen Harrop.

PARADE (*CLIMBER*)

Parentage   New Dawn Seedling × World's Fair
Breeder   Boerner 1953
Blooms   Deep pink to carmine; large, double; recurrent; light scent
Height and spread   10 × 6 ft (3 × 1.8 m)
Other uses   Pergolas

PARADE is a fast-growing, perpetual-flowering climber which does well on a cold sunless wall. It is vigorous with large, dark green leaves

NIGHT LIGHT (CLIMBER)

Synonym Poullight
Parentage Westerland × Pastorale
Breeder Poulsen 1982
Blooms Reddish buds opening to deep yellow; large, semi-double, produced in small clusters; recurrent; light scent
Height and spread 10 × 8 ft (3 × 2.4 m)
Other uses Pillars

NIGHT LIGHT is a vigorous, healthy rose; fast-growing with dark shiny leaves. It is a great asset for any garden.

DANSE DU FEU (CLIMBER)

Synonym Spectacular
Parentage Paul's Scarlet Climber × R. multiflora seedling
Breeder Mallerin 1954
Awards CM 1954
Blooms Orange scarlet; medium, double, produced in clusters; recurrent; moderate scent
Height and spread 8 × 8 ft (2.4 × 2.4 m)
Other uses Pillars

DANSE DU FEU's vivid red blooms rapidly turn to a burnished red. Very free-flowering throughout the season but slow to make an established plant. Stiffly branched with large dark green leaves. Enjoys both a north wall and full sun.

HANDEL (CLIMBER)

Synonym Macha
Parentage Columbine × Heidelberg
Breeder McGredy 1965
Awards TGC 1965
Blooms Creamy-white, edged bright rose pink; medium, long and pointed; classically shaped in clusters; recurrent; light scent
Height and spread 10 × 7 ft (3 × 2 m)
Other uses Pillars; prune to grow as a shrub; cut flowers

HANDEL is a long-flowering spectacular plant with very modern coloring. Upright growth and large, glossy, dark green leaves. Mildew and black spot can be a problem.

MORNING JEWEL (CLIMBER)

Parentage New Dawn × Red Dandy
Breeder Cocker 1968
Blooms Bright deep pink; medium-sized, semi-double; recurrent; moderate scent
Height and spread 12 × 8 ft (3.7 × 2.4 m)
Other uses Fences; pergolas

MORNING JEWEL is a useful plant which is extremely tough and produces very beautiful blooms. It is free-growing with shiny dark green foliage

CLIMBING THROUGH TREES

Strong-growing ramblers and climbers look sensational growing through and over trees.

Many gardens have trees which make very good supports for rambling roses. Growing these roses is a wonderful way to clothe old fruit trees, or camouflage old tree stumps, fallen trees or unsightly ruins. When growing strongly, rambling roses will need little maintenance and will smother the support with clouds of blooms, scenting the air with fragrance.

Little work is required other than the selection of well-suited varieties and the preparation of good planting positions. Avoid planting underneath a dense and broad evergreen or an all-enveloping oak tree, and choose a position on the sunny side of the tree. This should be far enough away from the trunk to allow a deep hole $3 \times 3 \times 3$ ft ($90 \times 90 \times 90$ cm) to be dug out and the soil to be replaced with a good, strong compost made up of 60 percent heavy loam, 25 percent peat, or peat substitute, and 15 percent very well-rotted, composted manure, to which is added two to three handfuls of good quality bonemeal. Line the sides of the hole with heavy-gauge polythene sheeting to deter intrusive surface roots from the tree. The roses should be planted in the late autumn to establish a good root system before the spring.

In many instances some form of support will be required to take new growth across to the trunk of the tree, such as a length of timber, or some wire. It will take a little time and patience to train the new shoots up into the branches, but once the roses have taken hold they will scramble skywards without any further assistance. They do not require pruning; an occasional mulch of well-rotted manure and a seasonal feed of a well-balanced rose fertilizer is all that is needed.

Growing roses through trees is an opportunity to use many of the more sprawling climbers and ramblers. For other varieties see pages 74–77 and pages 82–85.

◀ *A climbing rose cascades through an old apple tree covering the bare lower branches with an abundance of white blossom.*

▶ *"Wedding Day" is an ideal rose for growing over a tree as it is extremely vigorous and can cope with a shady site. Here it provides a stunning backdrop for the shrub rose "Reine des Violettes" and Salvia turkestanica.*

ALBERTINE *(RAMBLER)*

Parentage	R. wichuraiana × Mrs A. R. Waddell
Breeder	Barbier 1921
Blooms	Coppery buds opening into salmon pink flowers; large, double, loosely formed; summer-flowering; sweet scent
Height	20 ft (6 m)
Other uses	Pergolas

ALBERTINE is a very popular plant which produces a tremendous flush of color in mid-summer. It is an extremely vigorous plant with reddish young foliage followed by deep green leaves. It will sometimes attract mildew in the autumn and heavy rain can ruin the blooms.

BOBBY JAMES *(RAMBLER)*

Parentage	Multiflora seedling
Breeder	Sunningdale Nurseries 1961
Blooms	Creamy white; small, semi-double, produced in large clusters; summer-flowering; very good scent
Height	25 ft (7.5 m)
Other uses	Pergolas

BOBBY JAMES's very attractive foliage is an added bonus on this fast-growing rambler which has shiny dark leaves.

CLIMBING CÉCILE BRÜNNER *(CLIMBER)*

Synonym	Maltese rose
Parentage	Mutation of the bush variety
Breeder	Hosp 1894
Blooms	Light pink; exquisite, miniature, produced in large clusters; occasionally recurrent; light scent
Height	30 ft (9 m)
Other uses	Walls; pergolas

CLIMBING CÉCILE BRÜNNER, with careful tying and training, will produce a large show of perfectly formed small flowers which make good buttonholes. It is a very vigorous plant and if planted in a sunny position will produce a repeat show of color.

THE GARLAND *(RAMBLER)*

Parentage	R. moschata × R. multiflora
Breeder	Wells 1835
Blooms	White blush; very small, semi-double, produced in large clusters; summer-flowering; good scent
Height	15 ft (4.6 m)
Other uses	Fences; pergolas

THE GARLAND is useful for covering short trees and shrubs. It is a vigorous rambler with stiff stems and deep green foliage.

RAMBLING RECTOR (*RAMBLER*)

Parentage R. multiflora × R. moschata
Breeder Daisy Hill 1912
Blooms Creamy white, fading to pure
    white; small, double,
    produced in large clusters;
    summer-flowering; very good
    scent
Height 25 ft (7.5 m)
Other uses Pergolas

RAMBLING RECTOR is an extremely vigorous plant
and once encouraged to grow up a tree the
flower display is prodigious. Never prune, just
allow it to grow and grow.

ROSA FILIPES KIFTSGATE (*SPECIES*)

Parentage Mutation from R. filipes
Breeder Introduced by Murrell 1954
Blooms Creamy white; single,
    produced in large clusters;
    summer-flowering; scent
Height 32 ft (10 m)
Other uses Scrambling over fences

ROSA FILIPES KIFTSGATE is the fastest-growing
rambler available; stems can grow up to 10–15 ft
(3–4.6 m) in a season. It needs to become
established for 3–4 years before showing
color; a bonus is the myriad of small red hips.
The thorns are formidable and must be handled
with care.

ROSA LONGICUSPIS (*SPECIES*)

Parentage Sometimes mistaken for
    R. mulliganii
Origin Introduced before 1915
Blooms Milky white with yellow
    stamens; small, produced in
    large clusters; summer-
    flowering; light scent
Height 30 ft (9 m)
Other uses Pergolas

ROSA LONGICUSPIS is slightly slower growing than
some other ramblers but more than
compensates by producing masses of flowers
which will clothe the plant while still very
young. It also has very large leaves.

WEDDING DAY (*RAMBLER*)

Parentage Seedling of R. sinowilsonii
Breeder Stern 1950
Blooms White to blush; small, single,
    produced in clusters;
    summer-flowering; scent
Height 25 ft (7.5 m)
Other uses Pergolas

WEDDING DAY will grow in difficult situations
and thrives even in little sun. It is an extremely
vigorous plant with shiny mid-green leaves and
few thorns. The flowers are followed by small
yellow hips.

ARCHES AND PERGOLAS

Many of the more rampant ramblers and lax-growing climbers are perfect for training over arches and pergolas.

Arches and pergolas filled with color in mid-summer have been a gardener's dream since Victorian times, and at one time it was almost obligatory to have arches of roses spanning formal avenues. The introduction of the modern recurrent-flowering climber exposed the limitations of some of the older rambling and climbing varieties that bloom only once and, for a brief period, they became less popular. The pendulum has now swung back and the introduction of many new clematis varieties, some of which flower late in the season, has solved the problem of lack of color in late summer.

The tremendous advantage of growing roses on arches and pergolas is that it adds a vertical dimension to the garden and provides swathes of color that can be enjoyed without the formality of conventional rose beds. The varieties that excel on arches and pergolas have lax growth and flexible new branches which are easily tied in as they develop.

Pergolas and arches must be wide enough to allow for the passage of human traffic and to permit the plants to develop naturally. The overall width should be about 9 ft (2.7 m), with crossbars set about 8 ft (2.4 m) from the ground. These measurements on an extended pergola will give an attractive appearance. A pergola can be constructed in a wide range of materials. Ideally the supports to carry the lumber crossbars should be brick or stone pillars, not lumber which will deteriorate. If lumber has to be used throughout, it should be hardwood painted with a wood preservative. Metal arches are frequently used. Some rose growers prefer not to use metal supports in cold damp climates, believing that roses seem to dislike being secured to a cold, inhospitable frame.

The measurements for an arch will depend on its situation within the garden, but it should be at least 7 ft (2 m) high to allow access beneath it and a minimum of 4 ft 6 in (1.4 m) wide. Again avoid using metal; make the supports from timber and use polythene-coated wire to form the curved top.

Because of the lax growth associated with the majority of varieties suitable for arches and pergolas, it is very important that new shoots be tied in as they grow and that any pruning is carried out in the autumn well before the winter winds cause damage. All varieties benefit from regular feeding, particularly in the spring and early summer.

There are other climbing roses, in addition to those mentioned in this section, which will make marvellous colorful displays when grown on arches or over pergolas (see pages 74–81).

"Sanders' White Rambler" looks beautiful arching over an old gateway in the garden at Sissinghurst, Kent, England.

ALBERIC BARBIER (RAMBLER)

Parentage R. wichuraiana × Shirley Hibberd
Breeder Barbier 1900
Blooms Cream, small, double, produced in clusters; summer-flowering; light scent
Height and spread 15 × 12 ft (4.6 × 3.7 m)
Other uses Trees; weeping standards

ALBERIC BARBIER is a vigorous rambler with extremely lax growth that requires constant tying in. It will grow well in situations where there is little direct sunlight or where the conditions are poor. In a very warm position in the garden it will produce a good show of autumn color. It has dark glossy foliage which will last through most of the winter.

AMERICAN PILLAR (RAMBLER)

Parentage (R. wichuraiana × setigera) × red hybrid perpetual
Breeder Van Fleet 1902
Blooms Carmine with a white eye; medium-sized, produced in clusters; summer-flowering; very little scent
Height and spread 12 × 10 ft (3.7 × 3 m)
Other uses Walls; trees; pillars

AMERICAN PILLAR has been very popular but the cerise carmine blend can be difficult to accommodate in modern planting designs. It is a very vigorous plant which has an arching habit and large glossy leaves.

CLIMBING ICEBERG (CLIMBER)

Synonyms Fée des Neiges; Schneewittchen
Parentage Mutation from floribunda
Breeder Cant 1968
Award TGC 1969
Blooms White; medium-sized, produced in clusters; these are sometimes recurrent; light scent
Height and spread 10 × 10 ft (3 × 3 m)
Other uses Walls; pillars

CLIMBING ICEBERG is a useful plant because it responds well to early training. It is a vigorous climber with shiny, light green foliage. Heavy dead-heading will encourage some late flowers in the autumn.

EMILY GRAY (RAMBLER)

Parentage Jersey Beauty × Comtesse du Cayla
Breeder Williams 1918
Award GM 1916
Blooms Clear butter yellow; semi-double, produced in small clusters; summer-flowering; scent
Height 15 ft (4.6 m)
Other uses Pillars

EMILY GRAY is very useful as yellow ramblers are few and far between. Its brilliant color and attractive, almost evergreen foliage, which begins red and darkens to a glossy green, make it hard to resist. It grows moderately fast and has rather stiff stems.

FÉLICITÉ PERPÉTUE (*RAMBLER*)

Breeder	Jacques 1827
Blooms	Pure white; medium-sized, double rosettes, produced in large clusters; summer-flowering; sweet scent
Height and spread	12 × 10 ft (3.7 × 3 m)
Other uses	Pillars

FÉLICITÉ PERPÉTUE's large clusters of flowers are beautiful and long lasting. It is a vigorous plant with long slender stems and attractive foliage that is almost evergreen.

FRANÇOIS JURANVILLE (*RAMBLER*)

Parentage	R. wichuraiana × Mme Laurette Messimy
Breeder	Barbier 1906
Blooms	Salmon pink; medium-sized, double, produced in large clusters; summer-flowering; scent
Height and spread	20 × 15 ft (6 × 4.6 m)
Other uses	Trees

FRANÇOIS JURANVILLE is the ideal variety to smother a pergola. This tremendously vigorous rambler with extremely lax growth will require frequent tying in. It has small, dark green shiny leaves. In mild areas some flowers will appear in the autumn.

NEW DAWN (*CLIMBER*)

Synonym	Everblooming Dr W. Van Fleet
Parentage	Sport of Dr W. Van Fleet
Breeder	Somerset Rose Nurseries 1930
Blooms	Blush pink; medium-sized, double, produced in large clusters; recurrent; very good scent
Height and spread	10 × 8 ft (3 × 2.4 m)
Other uses	Pillars; shrub

NEW DAWN is a fascinating climber, famous for its adaptability and wonderful scent. It has medium-sized shiny leaves and grows vigorously. Although sometimes slow to become established, it will grow happily in difficult shaded corners.

NICE DAY (*MINIATURE CLIMBER*)

Synonyms	Chewsea; Patio Queen
Parentage	Sea Spray × Warm Welcome
Breeder	Warner 1994
Blooms	Soft salmon pink; true miniature, very double; produced in clusters; recurrent; sweet scent
Height and spread	8 × 6 ft (2.4 × 1.8 m)
Other uses	Pillars; shrub

NICE DAY is a very productive climber in true miniature fashion. Only light dead-heading is required. This is a free-flowering plant with small dense foliage.

PAUL'S SCARLET CLIMBER (RAMBLER)

Parentage	Seedling of Paul's Carmine Pillar
Breeder	Paul 1915
Award	GM 1915
Blooms	Bright red; medium-sized, double, produced in clusters; summer-flowering; slight scent
Height and spread	10 × 10 ft (3 × 3 m)
Other uses	Walls; pillars

PAUL'S SCARLET CLIMBER is a robust plant that has remained a favorite rose over many years. It is vigorous and free-flowering and has medium green foliage. It will grow in poor soil and dry conditions.

PHYLLIS BIDE (CLIMBER)

Parentage	Perle d'Or × W. A. Richardson
Breeder	Bide 1923
Award	GM 1924
Blooms	Yellow tinged with soft pink; small, semi-double, produced in clusters; recurrent; little scent
Height and spread	8 × 5 ft (2.5 × 1.5 m)
Other uses	Pillars; shrub

PHYLLIS BIDE is an old variety which has become popular again. It is slow-growing with small, glossy, dark leaves. It flowers prolifically.

MEG (CLIMBER)

Parentage	Paul's Lemon Pillar × Madame Butterfly
Breeder	Gosset 1954
Award	GM 1954
Blooms	Light apricot pink; single or semi-double, produced in small clusters; recurrent; good scent
Height and spread	12 × 12 ft (3.7 × 3.7 m)
Other uses	Walls

MEG will reward you with recurrent flushes of its beautiful blooms if planted against a wall that receives sun in autumn days. Tie the rigid stems in regularly to control the vigorous growth. It has large dark green leaves.

SANDERS' WHITE RAMBLER (RAMBLER)

Breeder	Sanders 1912
Blooms	Pure white; small, double, produced in large clusters; summer-flowering; good scent
Height and spread	12 × 12 ft (3.7 × 3.7 m)
Other uses	Pillars

SANDERS' WHITE RAMBLER is the ideal rambler to smother large structures. It enjoys extremely vigorous growth and young growth should be tied in as it develops. The vast quantity of blooms looks spectacular against its bright green foliage.

PILLARS AND TRIPODS

Climbing roses make splendid vertical features when grown up pillars, columns, and tripods.

Many rose gardens can be described as colorful but lacking in height variation. Although standard (tree) roses make interesting features when planted in mixed borders or among other roses, they can look formal and in many gardens are inappropriate because of their susceptibility to wind damage.

An excellent alternative is to grow climbing roses up pillars or, better still, an open-mesh column or a tall tripod. A simple pillar is easy to construct using good, well-preserved timber about 9 in (23 cm) square. For a pillar 6 ft (1.8 m) high use a length of wood about 8 ft (2.4 m) long, so that it can be anchored in the ground.

The aim when training plants is to encourage a good spread of color. If you are using a variety which quickly goes bare at the base, grow it up a pillar of open-mesh wire. Plastic-coated mesh is best since roses do not like being trained on bare metal. A length of open-mesh wire, 6 × 6– 8 × 8 ft (1.8 × 1.8–2.4 × 2.4 m), supported by one or two stout stakes, will produce a splendid pillar, against which up to three climbers can be grown. To ensure a good show of flowers, train young shoots to grow around the column, tying as many stems as possible horizontally. Alternatively, construct a tall tripod using good, strong, treated timber poles about 8 ft (2.4 m) in height. Sink the poles 18 in (46 cm) into the ground to anchor them securely, and bind the tops together with wire. A tripod will accommodate three plants. Whichever type is used, all supports for climbers or semi-ramblers must give ample space for the plants to develop, and all new growth should be well tied in to prevent wind damage.

There are some alternatives to the varieties described. These include "Compassion" and "Zéphirine Drouhin" (see pages 75–76), and "New Dawn" (see page 84).

A deep pink rose growing up a decorative white trelliswork pillar, topped by a finial, makes an interesting focal point. Wooden structures like this are ideal as roses do not like growing up cold metal.

ALOHA (CLIMBER)

Parentage Mercedes Gallart × New Dawn
Breeder Boerner 1949
Blooms Rose pink with deeper pink reverse; large, double and well shaped; recurrent; very good scent
Height and spread 8 × 8 ft (2.4 × 2.4 m)
Other uses Shrub

ALOHA is a very robust plant which is extremely free-flowering and very hardy. It will grow in very difficult positions where light is scarce. It is an upright grower with luxuriant foliage.

ALTISSIMO (CLIMBER)

Synonyms Delmur; Altus; Sublimely Single
Parentage Tenor seedling
Breeder Delbar – Chabert 1966
Blooms Deep bright red with prominent yellow stamens; very large, single, sometimes produced in clusters; recurrent; light scent
Height and spread 10 × 8 ft (3 × 2.4 m)
Other uses Walls; fences

ALTISSIMO's very large single blooms make it an eye-catching plant. They last a long time on the stem and heavy dead-heading will encourage a continuous show of flowers. It is a vigorous plant with large, very dark green leaves.

DORTMUND (CLIMBER)

Parentage Seedling × R. kordesii
Breeder Kordes 1955
Blooms Red with a white eye; single, produced in small clusters; recurrent; scent
Height and spread 10 × 6 ft (3 × 1.8 m)
Other uses Fences; pergolas; shrub

DORTMUND was one of the first recurrent-flowering Kordesii climbers to be bred. It is a semi-rambling, robust climber with dark glossy leaves. It will flourish in shady positions.

DREAMING SPIRES (CLIMBER)

Parentage Buccaneer × Arthur Bell
Breeder Mattock 1973
Award GM Belfast 1977
Blooms Clear yellow fading to pale yellow; large, double, produced in clusters; recurrent; good scent
Height and spread 12 x 8 ft (3.7 m × 2.4 m)
Other uses Walls

DREAMING SPIRES is a good variety which is adaptable to many situations in the garden. The pure yellow is a useful color in garden design. It grows vigorously and has large, dark green leaves.

D U B L I N   B A Y   (CLIMBER)

Synonym	Macdub
Parentage	Bantry Bay × Altissimo
Breeder	McGredy 1976
Awards	TGC 1974; BARB 1976
Blooms	Blood red; semi-double, produced in clusters; recurrent; scent
Height and spread	8 × 8 ft (2.4 × 2.4 m)
Other uses	Walls; shrub

DUBLIN BAY's bright color is a tremendous asset in the garden. Sometimes slow-growing to begin with, but it will, if very lightly pruned, develop into a large free-flowering plant with large, glossy, dark green leaves.

G O L D E N   S H O W E R S   (CLIMBER)

Parentage	Charlotte Armstrong × Captain Thomas
Breeder	Lammerts 1957
Award	AARS 1957
Blooms	Bright yellow turning pale yellow; large, semi-double, produced in clusters; recurrent; good scent
Height and spread	10 × 6 ft (3 × 1.8 m)
Other uses	Walls; shrub

GOLDEN SHOWERS is probably the most widely grown yellow climbing rose. It is slow-growing at first because of its very free-flowering nature. It has large, dark green leaves.

L A U R A   F O R D   (CLIMBER)

Synonym	Chewarvel
Parentage	Anna Ford × {Elizabeth of Glamis × (Galway Bay × Sutter's Gold)}
Breeder	Warner 1990
Award	GM 1988
Blooms	Yellow touched with pink; small, semi-double, produced in clusters; recurrent; scent
Height and spread	7 × 4 ft (2 × 1.2 m)
Other uses	Low walls; shrub

LAURA FORD is, technically, a miniature climber, one of a new strain which has great promise. It is a free-flowering semi-climber with small, dark, shiny leaves. No pruning is required and only light dead-heading.

W A R M   W E L C O M E   (CLIMBER)

Synonym	Chewizz
Parentage	{Elizabeth of Glamis × (Galway Bay × Sutter's Gold)} × Anna Ford)
Breeder	Warner 1991
Award	PIT 1988
Blooms	Orange-red, with a yellow eye; small, semi-double, produced in clusters; recurrent; scent
Height and spread	7 × 7 ft (2 × 2 m)
Other uses	Walls; shrub

WARM WELCOME is a modern short climber with beautiful small blooms. It is free-flowering with an arching habit and dark green leaves. Do not prune, but just dead-head lightly.

BANTRY BAY *(CLIMBER)*

Parentage	New Dawn × Korona
Breeder	McGredy 1967
Awards	CM 1967; CM Belfast 1969
Blooms	Pink; large, semi-double; recurrent; sweet scent
Height and spread	12 × 8 ft (3.7 × 2.4 m)
Other uses	Walls

BANTRY BAY's apple scent is very attractive. This rose is hardy enough to grow in the shade. It grows vigorously and has large leaves.

DELLA BALFOUR *(CLIMBER)*

Synonym	Harblend
Breeder	Harkness 1994
Blooms	Deep apricot pink; very large, double; recurrent; very good scent
Height and spread	8 × 6 ft (2.4 × 1.8 m)
Other uses	Walls; borders

DELLA BALFOUR, if very lightly dead-headed, will rapidly cover short fences and pillars with delightful lemon-scented blooms. It is slow-growing with large, deep green leaves.

HIGHFIELD *(CLIMBER)*

Synonym	Harcomp
Parentage	Sport of Compassion
Breeder	Harkness 1981
Blooms	Light yellow; large, double, produced in clusters; recurrent; very good scent
Height and spread	10 × 8 ft (3 × 2.4 m)
Other uses	Walls; borders

HIGHFIELD is a wonderful companion for its famous parent Compassion. It grows vigorously and has large dark green leaves.

HIGH HOPES *(CLIMBER)*

Synonym	Haryup
Parentage	Compassion × Congratulations
Breeder	Harkness 1992
Blooms	Light pink; well formed, double; recurrent; good scent
Height and spread	10 × 7 ft (3 × 2 m)
Other uses	Walls; pergolas; cut flowers

HIGH HOPES is a fast-growing climber with classic rose-shaped blooms produced on long stems. It will tolerate many situations in the garden. It has bushy, vigorous growth and handsome dark green foliage.

CONTAINERIZED BEAUTY

Patio roses and low-growing Floribundas will grow successfully in containers, proving the versatility of the rose.

The placement and planting of urns, troughs and other ornamental containers have long played a part in garden design. Container plants must be capable of thriving in a restricted space and limited amount of compost, and traditionally roses have not been the first choice for this popular style of gardening.

The main drawbacks to growing roses in containers are that they provide color for only half the year, and the root system of most varieties cannot be sustained within the confines of a pot or trough. The choice of variety is, therefore, vital. The most rewarding plants for pots are found among the patio roses and low-growing Floribundas. Some of the short, spreading ground-covers (see pages 130–137) are also very successful, especially if grown with a short standard in a large tub.

Choosing a suitable container is equally important. The capacity and shape of the container, and the material from which it is fashioned have a bearing on how well a rose will grow. The minimum amount of compost needed to sustain a patio rose is 12 in³ (30 cm³). The depth of the pot is more important than its length or width, and should be at least 12 in (30 cm). This is not always possible, particularly if using a window box, but the volume of compost must always be maintained. A container made of stone or prefabricated stone material suits roses best. This is because stone allows the roots to breathe and keeps them cooler than plastic. Plastic containers

Many patio roses are ideal for planting in a pot or container. They can be sited exactly where required – to brighten up a dull corner of the garden, for example.

should only be used in a temporary arrangement as, in the long term, the root system will suffer and may be destroyed through lack of air and, possibly, overheating. Weather-proofed lumber makes a good alternative to stone. If you make your own containers, protect the lumber with a plant-friendly preservative, applied at least a month before planting so that it is properly absorbed. Ground-cover roses are sometimes grown in hanging baskets; although the effect is very appealing, maintenance is extremely demanding and to achieve good results watering must be assiduous.

Fill your containers with good quality compost, such as John Innes Potting Compost No. 3. If you prefer to mix your own, combine 75 percent loam, 15 percent very well-rotted organic garden compost or aged manure, and 10 percent sharp sand. To give the roses a really good start in their container, add high-quality bonemeal and rose fertilizer according to the manufacturer's instructions.

Always water well, particularly in spring and summer. When you go on vacation rely on the goodwill of neighbors and friends, or install a reliable automatic watering system. An occasional foliar feed is essential and normal dead-heading and pruning must be carried out to keep the plants flowering well. Annual repotting is not essential, but it will pay dividends if you remove the top 3–4 in (7.5–10 cm) of compost in early spring and replace it with fresh compost of a similar type.

BABY MASQUERADE *(PATIO ROSE)*

Synonyms Tanba; Baby Maskarade; Baby Carnaval

Parentage Peon × Masquerade

Breeder Tantau 1956

Blooms Yellow, turning to pink and red as they age; small, double, produced in clusters; recurrent; very little scent

Height and spread 15 × 15 in (38 × 38 cm)

Other uses Standards

BABY MASQUERADE is an extremely free-flowering miniature that is a small replica of its parent. It has stood the test of time and is still tremendously popular. It has a bushy, open habit and small dark green leaves.

BALLERINA *(HYBRID MUSK)*

Breeder Bentall

Blooms Light pink with a white centre; single, produced in large clusters; recurrent; slight scent

Height and spread 4 × 3 ft (1.2 × 1 m)

Other uses Standards

BALLERINA is a remarkable plant that begins to flower in late mid-summer, producing masses of color reminiscent of phlox. Regular dead-heading will maintain plentiful blooms until late autumn. It makes bushy growth with an abundance of glossy, pale green leaves.

THE FAIRY *(MODERN SHRUB)*

Parentage Paul Crampel × Lady Gay

Breeder Bentall 1932

Blooms Clear rose pink; small, double, produced in large clusters; recurrent; slight scent

Height and spread 4 × 4 ft (1.2 × 1.2 m)

Other uses Borders; ground cover; standards

THE FAIRY flowers very freely from mid-summer until late autumn. If lightly pruned it will develop into a large sprawling plant with lax dense growth and small mid-green leaves.

GENTLE TOUCH *(PATIO ROSE)*

Synonym Diclulu

Parentage Liverpool Echo × (Woman's Own × Memento)

Breeder Dickson 1986

Award ROTY 1986

Blooms Pale pink; small, double, produced in clusters; recurrent; light scent

Height and spread 18 × 18 in (45 × 45 cm)

Other uses Standards

GENTLE TOUCH has been described as the definitive patio rose, with characteristic small leaves and flowers and a long flowering period. It is bushy with dark green foliage.

L I T T L E   B O - P E E P *(P A T I O   R O S E)*

Synonym Poullen
Parentage Caterpillar × seedling
Breeder Poulsen 1992
Award PIT 1991
Blooms Light pink; small, produced in dense clusters; recurrent; little scent
Height and spread 1½ × 1¾ ft (45 × 50 cm)
Other uses Containers; ground cover; standards

LITTLE BO-PEEP is a most interesting plant which will cover a patio with a myriad of small pink flowers and almost evergreen foliage. It has been described as a miniature shrub, being extremely bushy with small to medium leaves.

Q U E E N   M O T H E R *(P A T I O   R O S E)*

Synonyms Korquemu; Queen Mum
Parentage R. wichuraiana seedling × Toynbee Hall
Breeder Kordes 1991
Award TGS 1990
Blooms Clear pink; medium-sized, semi-double; recurrent; light scent
Height and spread 1½ × 1½ ft (45 × 45 cm)
Other uses Standards

QUEEN MOTHER is very free-flowering and could equally be described as a short Floribunda. The delicate color of its flowers is very complimentary to a gracious lady. It is very bushy and has dark green leaves.

L I T T L E   W H I T E   P E T *(P A T I O   R O S E)*

Synonym White Pet
Parentage Sport or seedling of Félicité Perpétue
Breeder Henderson 1879
Blooms White; small, double, produced in clusters; recurrent; scent
Height and spread 1½× 1¾ ft (45 × 50 cm)
Other uses Borders; standards

LITTLE WHITE PET is an old rose which has stood the test of time and is ideal for modern, small gardens. It is a bushy plant with very small, dark leaves and a slightly spreading habit. The almost snowball effect of the white flowers is ideal for brightening up dark corners.

Y E S T E R D A Y *(S M A L L   S H R U B)*

Synonym Tapis d'Orient
Parentage (Phyllis Bide × Shepherd's Delight) × Ballerina
Breeder Harkness 1974
Awards CM 1972
Blooms Lilac pink; small, double, produced in clusters; recurrent; good scent
Height and spread 1¾ × 1¾ ft (50 × 50 cm)
Other uses Low hedges; standards

YESTERDAY is the parent of many modern patio and ground-cover roses. The masses of flowers have an almost pale purple tint and are heavily scented. The leaves are small and glossy.

SWEET DREAM (PATIO ROSE)

Synonyms	Fryminicot; Sweet Dreams
Breeder	Fryer 1988
Awards	GM Belfast 1988; ROTY 1988
Blooms	Peachy apricot; medium-sized, very double, produced in large clusters; recurrent; light scent
Height and spread	1½ × 1 ft (45 × 30 cm)
Other uses	Low hedges; standards; exhibition

SWEET DREAM is one of the most successful patio roses and a great addition to the garden. It has an upright habit and plenty of glossy, deep green foliage. It will sometimes produce a much longer shoot which can be pruned.

SWEET MAGIC (PATIO ROSE)

Synonym	Dicmagic
Parentage	Peek A Boo × Bright Smile
Breeder	Dickson 1987
Awards	TGC 1986; ROTY 1987
Blooms	Orange with golden tints; small, double, produced in clusters; recurrent; strong scent
Height and spread	1½ × 1¼ ft (45 × 38 cm)
Other uses	Cut flowers; standard

SWEET MAGIC is probably the most widely grown patio rose. The perfect shape of the flowers makes it additionally appealing. It makes a very bushy plant with glossy foliage.

YVONNE RABIER (POLYANTHA)

Parentage	R. wichuraiana × Polyantha
Breeder	Turbat 1910
Blooms	White; small, double, produced in large clusters; recurrent; good scent
Height and spread	1¾ × 1¾ ft (50 × 50 cm)
Other uses	Low hedges; beds; standards

YVONNE RABIER is an old favorite which is easy to fit into the garden, either to blend with other plants or to brighten up a dull area. It has a delightful scent and the leaves are small and light green.

RED RASCAL (PATIO ROSE)

Synonym	Jacbed
Breeder	Warriner 1986
Blooms	Bright crimson; small, double, produced in small clusters; recurrent; little scent
Height and spread	1¼ × 1½ ft (38 × 45 cm)
Other uses	Borders; standards

RED RASCAL has a bushy habit and is disease-resistant. Its bright color makes it ideal for using as an accent plant in the garden.

MAKING A MINIATURE ROSE GARDEN

*You can design the perfect small-scale rose garden
with miniaturized roses.*

Small or miniaturized plants are very appealing and great satisfaction can be achieved by designing displays with them. Miniature roses have a valuable place in the garden, particularly in raised beds and borders and they will make admirable small rose beds of various shapes and sizes. A background planting of the new miniaturized climbers will complete a true Lilliputian scene.

Miniature gardens, and the use of roses in them, has now become almost an art form. One of the finest miniature rose gardens is the one at St. Anne's in Dublin (see page 154). Miniature rose-growing has also led to many societies promoting miniature rose exhibitions where the quality of the blooms and the way in which they are displayed are of the highest order.

When growing miniature roses the greatest attention must be paid to the quality and depth of the soil, and to the maintenance of the plants, just as for any other roses. When miniature roses were first introduced, some were criticized because they were prone to disease, particularly black spot. But time has shown that this problem occurred because miniature roses were being grown and treated as alpines, and their cultivation requirements were being neglected.

The average miniature makes a thoroughly presentable plant, some would say shrub, about 12 in (30 cm) high and often as wide. Small beds planted quite densely, with plants about 15 in (38 cm) apart, will give a very good effect. Miniatures must be pruned in the same way as their bigger cousins, that is removing about two-thirds of the top growth annually, and dead-heading quite severely in season.

The Royal National Rose Society's miniature rose garden. The roses are grown in raised beds and mini-standards add to the attractive composition.

ROULETTI (MINIATURE)

Synonym	Rosa chinensis minima
Breeder	Corevon 1922
Blooms	Pink; small, semi-double, produced in small clusters; recurrent; no scent
Height and spread	10 × 8 in (25 × 20 cm)
Other uses	Containers and window boxes

ROULETTI was the very first miniature rose to be introduced. It is a pretty, free-flowering plant which has tiny, pale green leaves.

BLACK JADE (MINIATURE)

Synonym	Benblack
Parentage	Sheri Anne × Laguna
Breeder	Bernadella 1985
Blooms	Dark velvety red with gold stamens; small, double; recurrent; little scent
Height and spread	15 × 10 in (38 × 25 cm)
Other uses	Containers and window boxes; exhibition

BLACK JADE is a great favorite on the show bench because its flowers are of consistently high quality. Bred by an enthusiastic amateur rose-breeder, it has an upright habit and small, dark leaves.

PARTY GIRL (MINIATURE)

Parentage	Rise 'n Shine × Sheri Anne
Breeder	Saville 1979
Blooms	Apricot yellow flushed with salmon pink; small; recurrent; slight scent
Height and spread	15 × 15 in (38 × 38 cm)
Other uses	Containers and window boxes; exhibition

PARTY GIRL is a low-growing, bushy miniature with well-shaped, pointed blooms. It is a popular show plant which regularly collects prizes.

JEAN KENNEALLY (MINIATURE)

Synonym	Tineally
Parentage	Futura × Party Girl
Breeder	Bennett 1984
Blooms	Apricot; small, double, produced in small clusters; good scent
Height and spread	18 × 12 in (45 × 30 cm)
Other uses	Containers and window boxes; exhibition

JEAN KENNEALLY is a very free-flowering variety. It has a bushy habit and is a good rose both for the garden and for exhibiting. It was bred by an amateur rose-breeder.

MAGIC CARROUSEL (MINIATURE)

Synonym Moorcar
Parentage Little Darling × Westmont
Breeder Moore 1972
Blooms Pale yellow with crimson edging; small, double, produced in clusters; recurrent; little scent
Height and spread 16 × 12 in (40 × 30 cm)
Other uses Standards; exhibition

MAGIC CARROUSEL is an extremely attractive plant with petite, globe-shaped blooms. It has a bushy habit and small glossy leaves.

ORANGE SUNBLAZE (MINIATURE)

Synonyms Meijikitar; Sunblaze
Breeder Meilland 1986
Blooms Vivid orange-red; small, double; recurrent; little scent
Height and spread 12 × 12 in (30 × 30 cm)
Other uses Containers and window boxes

ORANGE SUNBLAZE is a charming miniature which is extremely free-flowering and widely grown in pots and miniature gardens. It has compact, bushy growth and deep green foliage.

PEACHES 'N CREAM (MINIATURE)

Parentage Little Darling × Magic Wand
Breeder Woolcock 1976
Blooms Blend of cream and pink; small, double, produced in clusters; very little scent
Height and spread 17 × 12 in (43 × 30 cm)
Other uses Standards; exhibition

PEACHES 'N CREAM is very useful as a show plant and gains high awards for the color and quality of its flowers. It is hardy and vigorous and has dark green leaves.

RED ACE (MINIATURE)

Synonyms Amanda; Amruda
Parentage Scarletta × seedling
Breeder De Ruiter 1982
Blooms Dark crimson; small, semi-double, produced in clusters; recurrent; little scent
Height and spread 12 × 12 in (30 × 30 cm)
Other uses Containers and window boxes; cut flowers; exhibition

RED ACE is a useful color and has proved itself to be very adaptable to many situations. It is free-flowering with small dark green leaves.

RISE 'N SHINE (*MINIATURE*)

Synonyms   Golden Sunblaze; Golden
              Meillandina
Parentage Little Darling × Yellow Magic
Breeder   Moore 1977
Blooms   Bright yellow; small,
              produced in clusters;
              recurrent; very little scent
Height and spread 17 × 16 in (43 × 40 cm)
Other uses Exhibition

RISE 'N SHINE is a brilliant yellow variety which
is tremendously free-flowering and popular in
most rose-growing countries of the world. It has
deep green leaves but there is a certain
susceptibility to mildew.

SNOWBALL (*MINIATURE*)

Synonyms   Macangel; Angelita
Parentage Moana × Snow Carpet
Breeder   McGredy 1984
Blooms   White with a yellow base;
              very small, double, produced
              in clusters; recurrent; little
              scent
Height and spread 9 × 9 in (25 × 25 cm)
Other uses Containers and window
              boxes

SNOWBALL is an extremely small plant which is
permanently covered in tiny flowers. It is very
easy to grow from cuttings and forms a small,
round, compact plant with bright green leaflets.

STACEY SUE (*MINIATURE*)

Parentage Ellen Poulsen × Fairy
              Princess
Breeder   Moore 1976
Blooms   Shocking pink; small, double,
              produced in clusters;
              recurrent; little scent
Height and spread 12 × 12 in (30 × 30 cm)
Other uses Cut flowers

STACEY SUE is an ideal plant for small gardens
where space is at a premium. It has a bushy
habit and makes a very tough and robust plant
with pretty flowers and very glossy foliage.

GREEN DIAMOND (*MINIATURE*)

Parentage Seedling × Sheri Ann
Breeder   Moore 1975
Blooms   Greenish pink; very small,
              produced in clusters;
              recurrent; little scent
Height and spread 12 × 12 in (30 × 30 cm)
Other uses Cut flowers

GREEN DIAMOND is an attractive rose with
unusual coloring. It is a short, free-flowering
plant with dark green leaves. It achieves the
best color in cool conditions.

PATIO ROSES

Patio roses, with their compact growth and long flowering season, are ideal for small gardens.

The breeding of roses is developing all the time, probably more than for any other genus of garden plant. In the middle of the 20th century there was a dramatic increase in the flower power of roses, which also became more robust and disease-resistant. However, such plants were not necessarily suitable for small gardens.

Rose-breeders applied themselves to this problem and crossed some of the shorter-growing Hybrid Teas and Floribundas with miniature roses. They produced an entirely new type of plant, officially "short-growing cluster-flowering roses," but more popularly "patio roses" or in the USA "sweetheart roses." These are low-growing bush roses with miniaturized flowers and foliage, which are extremely free-flowering over a long period. The range of color is almost as wide as their larger cousins and they have a remarkable resistance to disease.

Patio roses are the product of a highly sophisticated breeding program and are designed to fit neatly into a small space. Their average height is about 18 in (45 cm), and many are as wide, with clusters of small, very double flowers. Although they are compact, they need the same ample feeding and seasonal maintenance as bush roses. Planted about 18 in (45 cm) apart, they can fill small beds in a most satisfying fashion.

Alternatively they will make very good, small, colorful hedges. They are also perfect to use as standard (tree) roses; propagated at about 18 in (45 cm) or 2 ft (60 cm), they are well suited to growing in this way and quickly add a new dimension to the small garden. There are now probably more than 40 patio roses available to the gardener, all bred in the last 30 years.

Recently there have been two major advances One is the appearance of taller plants with the same characteristics of small flowers and foliage and prodigious flower production; these have not been classified as yet but will probably be called "patio shrubs." The second is that some of the more lax-growing varieties are being considered as ground-cover plants.

"Anna Ford" is typical of patio roses with its perfect flower formation and tidy habit. With a height of about 18 in (45 cm), it is eminently suitable for small borders and containers.

ANNA FORD *(PATIO ROSE)*

Synonym Harpiccolo
Parentage Southampton × Darling Flame
Breeder Harkness 1980
Awards PIT 1981; GM Glasgow 1983
Blooms Vivid orange red with a yellow base; small, semi-double, produced in clusters; recurrent; little scent
Height and spread 18 × 12 in (45 × 30 cm)
Other uses Containers; cut flowers

ANNA FORD's color will add variety wherever it is planted. Growth is bushy with small, dark shiny leaves.If very lightly pruned it will grow into a small shrub.

BRIGHT SMILE *(PATIO ROSE)*

Classification Patio rose
Synonym Dicdance
Parentage Eurorose × seedling
Breeder Dickson 1980
Awards BARB 1980
Blooms Bright yellow; medium-sized, double; recurrent; moderate scent
Height and spread 18 × 18 in (45 × 45 cm)
Other uses Front of borders; containers

BRIGHT SMILE is a free-flowering, healthy plant with bright open flowers and attractive, bushy, dark shiny foliage.

CHATSWORTH *(PATIO ROSE)*

Synonym Tanotax
Parentage Seedling × seedling
Breeder Tantau 1995
Awards ROTY 1995
Blooms Rich pink, medium-sized, produced in large clusters; recurrent; slight scent
Height and spread 3 × 2 ft (90 × 60 cm)
Other uses Ground cover; standard

CHATSWORTH is a prodigious flower producer with remarkably disease-resistant, reddish-green foliage and arching stems.

TEAR DROP *(PATIO ROSE)*

Synonym Dicomo
Parentage Unknown
Breeder Dickson 1989
Blooms Blush white; small, semi-double, produced in clusters; recurrent; little scent
Height and spread 18 × 15 in (46 × 38 cm)
Other uses Containers and window boxes

TEAR DROP is a very useful plant in the garden with an interesting flower formation. It is a free-flowering bush with a profusion of small leaves.

TOP MARKS (PATIO ROSE)

Synonym Fryministar
Breeder Fryer 1992
Award GM 1990
Blooms Vivid orange-red; medium-sized, semi-double, perfectly formed, produced in clusters; recurrent; little scent
Height and spread 15 × 18 in (38 × 45 cm)
Other uses Containers and window boxes; standards

TOP MARKS has plentiful clusters of vivid flowers. It makes a bushy, compact plant with dark green shiny foliage, and may need protection from black spot.

BUTTONS (PATIO ROSE)

Synonym Dicmickey
Parentage (Liverpool Echo × Woman's Own) × Memento
Breeder Dickson 1987
Blooms Salmon pink; small, double, produced in clusters; recurrent; little scent
Height and spread 15 × 12 in (38 × 30 cm)
Other uses Containers and window boxes

BUTTONS' bright color is very useful in limited colour schemes. This plant has a bushy habit and small, dark green leaves.

BABY LOVE (PATIO ROSE)

Synonym Scrivluv
Parentage Sweet Magic × *R. davidii elongata* seedling
Breeder Scrivens 1994
Award GM 1993
Blooms Buttercup yellow; small to medium, single; recurrent; light scent
Height and spread 42 × 30 in (110 × 75 cm)
Other uses Standards; containers and window boxes

BABY LOVE was bred as a disease-resistant rose and is rapidly becoming a very adaptable plant in the garden. It is shrubby with small leaves.

EMILY LOUISE (PATIO ROSE)

Synonym Harwilla
Parentage Judy Garland × Anna Ford
Breeder Harkness 1988
Award CM 1988
Blooms Yellow turning pink as they age; small, single, produced widely spaced in clusters; recurrent; light scent
Height and spread 18 × 24 in (45 × 60 cm)
Other uses Containers and window boxes; borders

EMILY LOUISE is a very pretty plant with open flowers. It has a bushy yet slightly spreading habit and shiny dark green foliage.

F ESTIVAL (PATIO ROSE)

Synonym	Kordialo
Parentage	Regensberg × seedling
Breeder	Kordes 1994
Awards	TGC 1993; ROTY 1994
Blooms	Crimson scarlet with silvery white on the reverse side; medium-sized, semi-double, produced in clusters; recurrent; light scent
Height and spread	24 × 18 in (60 × 45 cm)
Other uses	Standard

FESTIVAL grows evenly, with a dense bushy habit and deep green, medium-sized leaves. It produces a blaze of color throughout the summer and autumn.

C IDER C UP (PATIO ROSE)

Synonym	Dicladida
Parentage	Memento × seedling
Breeder	Dickson 1988
Blooms	Deep apricot pink; small, well-formed, produced in clusters; recurrent; moderate scent
Height and spread	15 × 12 in (38 × 30 cm)
Other uses	Containers and window boxes; cut flowers

CIDER CUP is a beautiful and very popular variety which is frequently used as a cut flower in small arrangements. It is bushy and upright with small leaves.

M INILIGHTS (PATIO ROSE)

Synonym	Dicmoppet
Parentage	White Spray × Bright Smile
Breeder	Dickson 1988
Award	TGC 1985
Blooms	Pale gold; small, single, produced in clusters; recurrent; little scent
Height and spread	18 × 18 in (45 × 45 cm)
Other uses	Containers and window boxes

MINILIGHTS has large clusters of very small simple flowers, which are enjoyable for their profusion and continuity. It is bushy, with a slightly spreading habit and small leaves.

P EEK A B OO (PATIO ROSE)

Synonyms	Dicgrow; Brass Ring
Parentage	Memento × Nozomi
Breeder	Dickson 1981
Award	CM 1981
Blooms	Apricot fading to pink; small, double, produced in clusters; recurrent; little scent
Height and spread	18 × 18 in (45 × 45 cm)
Other uses	Containers and window boxes; cut flowers

PEEK A BOO is a typical patio rose, with well-formed small blooms which can be used for floral decorations. It has an upright habit and small dark green leaves.

REGENSBERG (*PATIO ROSE*)

Synonyms Macyoumis; Buffalo Bill; Young Mistress

Parentage Geoff Boycott × Old Master

Breeder McGredy 1979

Award BARB 1979

Blooms White center shading to pink; medium-sized, double, produced in clusters; recurrent; little scent

Height and spread 2 × 2 ft (60 × 60 cm)

Other uses Borders; standards

REGENSBERG is a very interesting and, with its unique blend of pink and white, theatrically colored plant. A positive contribution to the world of roses from the "hand-painted" series, it is free-flowering and very bushy with glossy, bright green foliage.

PENELOPE KEITH (*PATIO ROSE*)

Synonyms Macfreego; Free Gold

Breeder McGredy 1984

Award TGC 1984

Blooms Golden yellow with tinge of pink; perfectly shaped, produced in clusters; recurrent; slight scent

Height and spread 2 × 1 ft (60 × 30 cm)

Other uses Cut flowers

PENELOPE KEITH has well-shaped blooms which are carried on relatively long stems. It is an upright, compact plant with small, bright green leaves, and makes a good short bedding plant.

MANDARIN (*PATIO ROSE*)

Synonym Korcelin

Award GM Dublin 1987

Blooms Deep pink tinged with orange yellow; small, double, produced in clusters; little scent

Height and spread 1½ × 1½ ft (45 × 45 cm)

Other uses Standards; exhibition

MANDARIN can more properly be described as a tall miniature. It is very free-flowering, with a large number of perfect Hybrid Tea-shape small blooms. The habit is bushy and the foliage medium green.

PRETTY POLLY (*PATIO ROSE*)

Synonyms Meitonje; Pink Symphony; Sweet Sunblaze

Parentage Coppélia × Magic Carrousel

Breeder Meilland 1989

Award PIT 1989

Blooms Light pink; medium-sized, double; recurrent; light scent

Height and spread 1½ × 1½ ft (45 × 45 cm)

Other uses Containers and window boxes; front of borders

PRETTY POLLY is a small plant, ideally suited for both borders and pots. It has a dense, robust habit and disease-resistant foliage.

S TARINA (PATIO ROSE)

Synonym Meigabi
Parentage (Dany Robin × Fire King) ×
Perla de Montserrat
Breeder Meilland 1965
Blooms Orange-red; small, produced
in small clusters; recurrent;
light scent
Height and spread 1½ × 1¼ ft (45 × 38 cm)
Other uses Containers and window
boxes; exhibition

STARINA is a small bushy plant with glossy foliage. It makes a very good display and is also disease-resistant.

M ARIE P AVIÉ (PATIO ROSE)

Synonym Marie Pavier
Breeder Alégatière 1888
Blooms White; small, double,
produced in clusters;
recurrent; scent
Height and spread 2 × 1¼ ft (60 × 50 cm)
Other uses Borders; containers and
window boxes

MARIE PAVIÉ is an old rose which has become very popular again today. A vigorous variety which always seems to be in flower.

C LARISSA (PATIO ROSE)

Synonym Harpocrustes
Parentage Southampton × Darling
Flame
Breeder Harkness 1985
Award TGC 1981
Blooms Pale apricot; small, produced
in clusters; recurrent; little
scent
Height and spread 2 × 1½ ft (60 × 45 cm)
Other uses Containers and window
boxes; cut flowers

CLARISSA has well-shaped flowers set off by small, leathery, dark leaves. The soft coloring makes this a useful variety for flower arrangers.

I NTERNATIONAL H ERALD T RIBUNE (PATIO ROSE)

Synonyms Harquantum, Violetta, Viorita
Parentage R. californica seedling
Breeder Harkness 1985
Award GM Geneva 1986
Blooms Violet purple; semi-double,
produced in clusters;
recurrent; slight scent
Height and spread 1½ × 1¼ ft (45 × 40 cm)
Other uses Containers and window
boxes; standards

INTERNATIONAL HERALD TRIBUNE's unusual deep color adds originality to a rose border. The flowers are complemented by the dark foliage.

ROSES IN BEDS

*For sheer magnificence, few sights in the garden can
exceed a bed of roses in full bloom.*

The classic large-flowered Hybrid Tea is everyone's idea of the perfect rose, and the one we most associate with growing in beds. Modern Hybrid Tea roses are the culmination of the rose hybridist's art, brought to perfection in the twentieth century. Over the past 90 years the health of the plants has been significantly improved. In addition, the range of colors has widened and now includes not only white, pinks, reds and yellows, but also oranges, vermilions, bicolors and blends. In the past, the strongest criticism levelled at these roses was their lack of scent. Now this defect has been addressed by the breeders and many new varieties not only have the exquisite flower form but are also wonderfully fragrant.

Hybrid Teas need space and grow best unimpeded by any other plants. They respond to regular feeding and benefit from generous mulching with organic material in spring. Avoid dense ground-cover planting as it will compete with the roses, to their detriment. The temptation in a small garden is to pack plants rather too closely together, so although Hybrid Teas can enhance a small space they are better planted in large beds. This not only gives a more eye-catching display, but also allows for a more generous spacing between plants.

Bushes should be planted about 2 ft (60 cm) apart and not more than four deep (across the width of the bed). This

Although Hybrid Teas grow best unimpeded by other plants, the Alchemilla mollis *shown here is low-growing and will not prevent the light from reaching the rose bushes.*

means that a well-planted bed should measure about 9 ft (2.7 m) wide and, ideally, have a 18 in (45 cm) margin around the edge. This spacing enables the gardener to keep the bed weed-free and spray the bushes against pests and diseases without damaging the plants. The length of the bed is a matter of proportion, but bear in mind that you will be tempted to take short cuts through a long bed. If you have a long area to fill, several shorter beds will be more practical than one long one. Round or oval beds are very attractive provided you are willing to put some effort into keeping the edges neat (mowing around a curve is slightly more tricky than mowing in a straight line).

Inevitably, two criticisms are made of large beds of Hybrid Tea roses: they are all the same height and they lack color out of season. The first point can be solved by adding pillars of color (see pages 86–89), but a more sophisticated and attractive alternative is to plant a formal grouping of bushes with standard (tree) roses (see pages 146–147). To provide interest when the roses are not in flower, plant early-flowering bulbs, principally daffodils, to give color. They can be arranged in clumps, but take care they never deprive the roses of light, which in early spring is an absolute necessity. Spring bedding, such as pansies or daisies, can be planted around the perimeter.

DAWN CHORUS (HYBRID TEA)

Synonym Dicquaser
Parentage Wishing × Peer Gynt
Breeder Dickson 1993
Awards ROTY 1993; BARB 1993; GM Dublin 1994
Blooms Deep orange; medium-sized, double, with a perfect shape, produced in small clusters; recurrent; light scent
Height and spread 30 × 24 in (75 × 60 cm)
Other uses Standards

DAWN CHORUS makes a neat bush and is a modern-looking variety with beautifully formed flowers in a strong color. The deep green, disease-free foliage, which can be almost reddish, complements the blooms very well.

ALEC'S RED (HYBRID TEA)

Synonym Cored
Parentage Fragrant Cloud × Dame de Coeur
Breeder Cocker 1970
Awards EM 1969; PIT 1970; Fragrance Belfast 1972; ADR 1973
Blooms Cherry red; large, double; recurrent; excellent scent
Height and spread 3 × 2 ft (90 × 60 cm)
Other uses Standards; exhibition

ALEC'S RED is an extremely popular variety which has been a garden favorite for many years. The large, well-formed blooms turn a deeper red as they age and have a most attractive scent. It is a vigorous, upright bush with large dark green leaves, and is sometimes prone to mildew.

ELINA (HYBRID TEA)

Synonyms Dicjana; Peaudouce
Parentage Nana Mouskouri × Lolita
Breeder Dickson 1983
Awards CM 1983; SM Glasgow 1985; ADR 1987; NZ GM 1987; JM 1994
Blooms Ivory with a lemon centre; very large, double, with a perfect shape; scent
Height and spread 42 × 30 in (110 × 75 cm)
Other uses Standards

ELINA is a fantastic producer of quality blooms and probably the most underrated rose of the 1980s. It will outlive rivals for many years to come and is the crowning achievement of one of the oldest rose-breeding houses in the world. It has a vigorous, bushy habit and luxurious, deep green foliage.

FRAGRANT CLOUD (HYBRID TEA)

Synonyms Tanellis; Duftwolke; Nuage Parfumé
Parentage Seedling × Prima Ballerina
Breeder Tantau 1963
Awards PIT 1964; GM Portland 1966; World's Favourite Rose 1972
Blooms Dusky scarlet; very large, well-shaped; excellent scent
Height and spread 30 × 30 in (75 × 75 cm)
Other uses Standards

FRAGRANT CLOUD explodes the myth that modern roses do not have a scent. It flowers very early with large, high-centered blooms that turn slightly purple with age. It is vigorous and bushy with large, deep green leaves prone to mildew in the autumn.

FREEDOM (HYBRID TEA)

Synonym	Dicjem
Parentage	(Eurorose × Typhoon) × Bright Smile
Breeder	Dickson 1984
Awards	GM 1983; CM Glasgow 1985; GM The Hague 1992
Blooms	Rich yellow; medium-sized, double, produced in small clusters; recurrent; light scent
Height and spread	30 × 24 in (75 × 60 cm)
Other uses	Standards

FREEDOM is a modern yellow rose that is extremely free-flowering and weatherproof. It is bushy with an abundance of glossy green foliage which is a perfect foil for the bright color of the flowers.

GRANDPA DICKSON (HYBRID TEA)

Synonym	Irish Gold
Parentage	(Perfecta × Gov Braga de Cruz) × Piccadilly
Breeder	Dickson 1966
Awards	PIT 1965; Golden Rose of The Hague 1966; GM Belfast 1969; GM Portland 1970
Blooms	Light lemon yellow, large, double; recurrent; light scent
Height	3 ft (90 cm)
Other uses	Exhibition

GRANDPA DICKSON is named after the head of the Dickson family and is a fitting tribute to a legendary rose-grower. The freedom from disease and perfectly formed large blooms have made this a garden favorite for many years. In hot weather the flowers become flushed with pink. It has a very upright habit and distinctive light green foliage.

INGRID BERGMAN (HYBRID TEA)

Synonym	Poulman
Parentage	Precious Platinum
Breeder	Poulsen 1984
Awards	TGC 1983; GM Belfast 1986; GM Madrid 1986; Golden Rose of The Hague 1987
Blooms	Dark red; large, double; recurrent; faint scent
Height and spread	30 × 24 in (75 × 60 cm)
Other uses	Standards

INGRID BERGMAN has leathery, dark green, disease-resistant foliage complementing a deep red rose that is very free-flowering. The lack of scent does not detract from this very hardy upright-growing bedding variety.

JUST JOEY (HYBRID TEA)

Parentage	Fragrant Cloud × Dr A. J. Verhage
Breeder	Cant 1973
Awards	JM 1986; World's Favorite Rose 1994
Blooms	Coppery pink turning to buff as they age; large, double, becoming frilly around the edge as they age; strong scent
Height and spread	30 × 24 in (75 × 60 cm)
Other uses	Standards

JUST JOEY is an extraordinary rose. The blooms have a great intensity of copper pink which turns buff as they age. The plant requires plenty of feeding to obtain large blooms. It has a bushy habit with deep green foliage.

KEEPSAKE (HYBRID TEA)

Synonyms	Kormalda; Esmeralda
Parentage	Seedling × Red Planet
Breeder	Kordes 1981
Awards	TGC 1980; GM Portland 1987
Blooms	Deep pink shades; very large, beautifully shaped, very free; recurrent; medium scent
Height and spread	3 × 2 ft (90 × 60 cm)
Other uses	Standards; exhibition

KEEPSAKE is an outstandingly robust plant which produces large, good-quality blooms when disbudded. Quite a late flowering rose, it will benefit from light pruning and copious feeding. It makes very strong, bushy growth and has dark foliage.

PASCALI (HYBRID TEA)

Synonyms	Lenip; Blanche Pascal
Parentage	The Queen Elizabeth Rose × White Butterfly
Breeder	Lens 1963
Awards	CM 1963; GM The Hague 1963; AARS 1969; GM Portland 1967
Blooms	Pure white; medium-sized, double; little scent
Height	30 in (75 cm)
Other uses	Cut flowers; standards

PASCALI is a white rose of considerable brilliance with few equals. The long, pointed buds develop into well-shaped blooms that have a great resistance to the rain. A most reliable variety, it is an upright grower, very free-flowering and has dark green foliage. In 1991 it was voted the World's Favorite Rose.

PAUL SHERVILLE (HYBRID TEA)

Synonyms	Harqueterwife; Heart Throb
Parentage	Compassion × Mischief
Breeder	Harkness 1983
Awards	EM 1982; CM Glasgow and Belfast 1984; Auckland Fragrance 1991
Blooms	Salmon pink shades; large, double, single and in clusters, recurrent; strong scent
Height and spread	30 × 30 in (75 × 75 cm)
Other uses	Standards

PAUL SHERVILLE is a bushy plant that could equally be described as a Floribunda or a shrub. It always seems to be in flower and is highly valued for its scent. It makes very bushy growth, has dark, strong foliage and is very disease-resistant.

PICCADILLY (HYBRID TEA)

Synonym	Macar
Parentage	McGredy's Yellow × K. Herbst
Breeder	McGredy 1959
Awards	CM 1959; GM Madrid 1960; GM Rome 1960
Blooms	Scarlet with a yellow reverse; medium-sized, double or single or in small clusters; recurrent; light scent
Height and spread	30 × 24 in (75 × 60 cm)
Other uses	Standards

PICCADILLY has long been described as the definitive bicolor. This free-flowering, bright, early rose has had many imitators but no equals. A bed of Piccadilly is a memorable sight. It has a bushy habit with dark green foliage and is slightly prone to mildew.

SIMBA (HYBRID TEA)

Synonyms	Korbelma; Goldsmith; Helmut Schmidt
Parentage	Korgold × seedling
Breeder	Kordes 1981
Award	TGC 1979
Blooms	Clear buttercup yellow; large, double, perfectly shaped; recurrent; strong scent
Height and spread	2½ × 2½ ft (75 × 75 cm)
Other uses	Standards

SIMBA has been described as the perfect yellow bedding rose. An even grower with a great continuity of flower, it has a bushy habit and large dark green leaves.

SILVER JUBILEE (HYBRID TEA)

Parentage	Seedling × Mischief
Breeder	Cocker 1978
Awards	PIT 1977; JM 1985; GM Belfast 1989; BARB 1978
Blooms	Rosy salmon outer petals shading to peach pink tinged with apricot at the centre; large, double; recurrent; light scent
Height and spread	3½ × 2 ft (110 × 60 cm)
Other uses	Standards; exhibition

SILVER JUBILEE is a quite remarkable, robust variety with high-quality blooms and considered by many to be *the* rose of the 1980s. The flowering stems are short which makes for a neat bush. It has a vigorous, bushy habit with deep green, leathery foliage.

TEQUILA SUNRISE (HYBRID TEA)

Synonym	Dicobey Beaulieu
Parentage	Bonfire Night × Freedom
Breeder	Dickson 1989
Awards	GM 1988; GM Belfast 1991; SM Glasgow 1992; CM Dublin 1992
Blooms	Yellow edged with scarlet; medium-sized, produced in small clusters; light scent
Height and spread	2½ × 2 ft (75 × 60 cm)
Other uses	Standards

TEQUILA SUNRISE is a dramatic and eye-catching blend of bright yellow and scarlet. It is a bushy, disease-resistant plant with dark glossy leaves.

TROIKA (HYBRID TEA)

Synonyms	Poumidor; Royal Dane
Parentage	(Super Star × seedling) × Hanne
Breeder	Poulsen 1971
Awards	GM 1973; JM 1992
Blooms	Orange-bronze and reddish-orange; large, double; recurrent; strong scent
Height and spread	3 × 2 ft (90 × 60 cm)
Other uses	Standards

TROIKA is a useful variety, extremely tolerant of alkaline soils. Its vigor in very warm climates is legendary and it can easily grow to 6–8 ft (1.8–2.4 m). It is a disease-resistant plant with luxuriant, bright green foliage.

MISTER LINCOLN (HYBRID TEA)

Parentage Chrysler Imperial × Charles Mallerin
Breeder Swim and Weeks 1964
Award AARS 1965
Blooms Dark velvety red; very large, double; recurrent; strong scent
Height and spread 4 × 2 ft (120 × 60 cm)
Other uses Borders; exhibition

MISTER LINCOLN is a popular rose for the garden and also for showing. It produces large, pointed buds which open to reveal richly colored blooms of colossal size. It has an upright habit and grows vigorously. The large leaves are a perfect foil for the flowers.

BLESSINGS (HYBRID TEA)

Parentage Queen Elizabeth × seedlings
Breeder Gregory 1968
Awards CM 1968
Blooms Rosy salmon pink; large, double; recurrent; scent
Height and spread 3 × 2½ ft (90 × 75 cm)
Other uses Standards

BLESSINGS has been described as the ideal bedding rose because it flowers continuously from early in the season until late autumn. It has a neat, bushy habit and large leaves which provide a good background to the delicately tinted blooms.

PEER GYNT (HYBRID TEA)

Parentage Colour Wonder × Golden Giant
Breeder Kordes 1968
Awards CM 1967; GM Belfast 1969
Blooms Bright yellow with red tinges in the bud; large, double, produced in clusters; recurrent; light scent
Height and spread 3 × 2 ft (90 × 60 cm)
Other uses Cut flowers; exhibition

PEER GYNT is a very free-flowering variety which has proved itself to be remarkably hardy and tolerant of poor soils. It requires disbudding to obtain blooms large enough for showing. The plant grows vigorously and has a bushy habit. Mildew is sometimes a problem in the autumn.

SUPER STAR (HYBRID TEA)

Synonyms Tanostar; Tropicana
Parentage (Seedling × Peace) × (Seedling × Alpine Glow)
Breeder Tantau 1960
Award PIT 1960
Blooms Vermilion; medium-sized, produced in small clusters; recurrent; scent
Height and spread 3 × 3 ft (90 × 90 cm)
Other uses Cut flowers

SUPER STAR was the first of the brilliant vermilion bush roses and is still very popular for its stunning color and upright habit. The plant is prone to mildew.

T O U R N A M E N T O F R O S E S (H Y B R I D T E A)

Synonyms	Jacient, Poesie
Breeder	Warriner 1989
Awards	AARS 1989; CM Belfast 1990
Blooms	Light salmon pink; large, double; some scent
Height and spread	3½ × 2 ft (110 × 60 cm)
Other uses	Standards

TOURNAMENT OF ROSES is very free-flowering with an upright habit. The attractive blooms are set off well by the dark, glossy leaves. This rose is popular in many parts of the world.

P A R A D I S E (H Y B R I D T E A)

Synonyms	Wezeip, Burning Sky, Passion
Breeder	Weeks 1978
Award	AARS 1979
Blooms	Opalescent lavender and magenta pink; large, double; good scent
Height and spread	3 × 1½ ft (90 × 45 cm)
Other uses	Cut flowers; exhibition

PARADISE's distinct coloring makes it an interesting rose to have in the garden. The deep green foliage may occasionally attract some mildew.

P R I S T I N E (H Y B R I D T E A)

Synonym	Jacpico
Parentage	White Masterpiece × First Prize
Breeder	Warriner 1978
Awards	EM and CM 1979; CM Belfast 1981
Blooms	Ivory, blushed pink; very large, double; heavily scented
Height and spread	3½ × 2½ ft (110 × 75 cm)
Other uses	Cut flowers

PRISTINE has very large blooms produced on a strong plant with handsome, large, dark leaves. This is one of the perfect white roses and other excellent whites have been bred from it. The wonderful scent is an added attraction.

R E D D E V I L (H Y B R I D T E A)

Synonyms	Dicam; Coeur d'Amour
Parentage	Silver Lining × Prima Ballerina
Breeder	Dickson 1967
Awards	CM 1965; GM Belfast 1969
Blooms	Medium red; large, double; recurrent; scent
Height and spread	4 × 3 ft (120 × 90 cm)
Other uses	Exhibition

RED DEVIL is probably the finest and most consistent producer of large, prize-winning blooms. It requires disbudding and some protection in wet weather to develop immaculate, large flowers. This is a strong-growing, bushy rose with glossy foliage.

DOUBLE DELIGHT (*HYBRID TEA*)

Synonym Andeli
Parentage Granada × Garden Party
Breeder Swim and Ellis 1977
Awards GM Rome 1976; AARS 1977; World's Favourite Rose 1985
Blooms Blush, flushed carmine; large, double; recurrent; strong scent
Height and spread 2 × 1½ ft (60 × 45 cm)
Other uses Exhibition

DOUBLE DELIGHT has large blooms with perfect reflexed petals that compensate for an uneven bush. It is widely grown and has many devoted admirers but is prone to mildew.

SAVOY HOTEL (*HYBRID TEA*)

Synonyms Harvintage; Integrity;
Parentage Silver Jubilee × Amber Queen
Breeder Harkness 1989
Awards GM Dublin 1988; CM Belfast 1990
Blooms Light pink with deeper tones; very large, double, recurrent; light scent
Height and spread 3 × 2 ft (90 × 60 cm)
Other uses Standards; cut flowers

SAVOY HOTEL is a recent addition to the ranks of large Hybrid Teas; its perfect form is a great attraction to exhibitors and cut-flower enthusiasts. It is an early-flowering, vigorous plant and blooms freely. The flowers are borne singly on short stems.

VALENCIA

Synonym Koreklia
Breeder Kordes 1989
Awards Edland 1989; CM 1989
Blooms Buff orange with gold shadings; very large, double; strong scent
Height and spread 3 × 2 ft (90 × 60 cm)
Other uses Exhibition

VALENCIA has pure amber, very large flowers that are quite startling in their luminosity and are well complemented by the bronze-green foliage. This very reliable bedding plant is bushy and disease-resistant, and the excellent scent is a further attraction. The petals can sometimes be damaged by persistent rain.

PURE BLISS (*HYBRID TEA*)

Synonym Dictator
Parentage Elina × seedling
Breeder Dickson 1994
Awards SM Genoa
Blooms Pale pink; large; recurrent; strong scent
Height and spread 3 × 2 ft (90 × 60 cm)
Other uses Standards; exhibition

PURE BLISS is a most beautiful free-flowering variety with a great future. It has a bushy habit and is disease-resistant.

ROSES IN BORDERS

Old Garden Roses, with their huge quantities of sumptuous blooms, have a very special place in a summer border.

Nowadays, few ancestors of modern plant cultivars continue to be grown widely and to make a valuable contribution to our borders. However, many shrub rose varieties, such as the Gallicas, Damasks, Albas and Centifolias, are as well loved today as they were 500 years ago when they were grown in monastic gardens and the grounds of great houses, and by herbalists. The Bourbons and Hybrid Perpetuals bring a touch of pure Victoriana to a border and, unlike many Old Garden Roses, have the advantage of repeat-flowering. Some of the scented varieties, such as "Louise Odier" and "Reine de Violettes" (see pages 116-117), are quite exceptional.

All these groups of roses make fine border plants with their attractive foliage and form. However, the moss roses are less suitable and need to be placed with care. Although the mossy stems and sepals are fascinating and the summer flowers are magnificent, once these are spent, the plants contribute little to a border.

There is a multitude of Old Garden Roses to choose from and the catalogues can make intriguing reading. However, because of their diversity no simple collective description can be given as with other rose groups. A good rule of thumb is to assume that most will form shrubs about 4–5 ft (1.2– 1.5 m) tall and almost the same distance across. Try to avoid crowding the base with other plants or the benefits of early season sunlight will be lost.

It is important to remember that most of the roses introduced before 1800 form medium to large shrubs and flower only in summer. To achieve the finest effect with these roses, plant them in groups; three or five plants of the same variety, spaced about 3 ft (1 m) apart, will give a good display. Many Old Garden Roses look their best in large borders where they can be mixed with groups of recurrent-flowering modern shrubs and Floribundas which continue to provide color in the border well into autumn.

Old Garden Roses have very few pruning requirements; simply remove dead heads regularly, taking a generous length of stem when you do so. Damasks and Gallicas benefit from pruning out the odd large stem that has become too woody immediately after flowering. This will encourage new growth and provide plenty of flowering wood for the following summer. Take care not to cut back this new wood in spring simply because some of these young stems appear rather upright. If you leave them they will eventually bend under the weight of the blooms.

Old Garden Roses need generous feeding to do well. The majority do not succumb to the ravages of black spot, but some varieties are susceptible to unsightly mildew. Take routine measures against aphid attack.

![Old Garden Roses flourish in a mixed border at Mottisfont Abbey, Hampshire, in England]

Old Garden Roses flourish in a mixed border at Mottisfont Abbey, Hampshire, in England, where their subtle coloring combines well with other plants. Many such varieties are also wonderfully scented.

FRAU KARL DRUSCHKI (HYBRID PERPETUAL)

Synonyms	Reine de Neiges; Snow Queen; White American Beauty
Parentage	Merveille de Lyon × Madame Caroline Testout
Breeder	Lambert 1901
Blooms	Pure white; large, double; recurrent; little scent
Height and spread	6 × 4 ft (1.8 × 1.2 m)
Other uses	Semi-climber

FRAU KARL DRUSCHKI is a rose famous for its pure white blooms. It has long, rather rambling stems which can be left to form a large, spreading plant or trained against a trellis. Prolonged wet weather spoils the blooms.

TUSCANY SUPERB (GALLICA)

Synonym	Double Velvet
Parentage	Sport from Tuscany
Breeder	Paul 1848
Blooms	Velvety red; large, semi-double, open, produced in small clusters; summer-flowering; very strong scent
Height and spread	3 × 3 ft (1 × 1 m)
Other uses	Bush

TUSCANY SUPERB has beautiful velvety red flowers with prominent yellow stamens. It makes a strong, rounded bush with dark green foliage.

WILLIAM LOBB (MOSS)

Synonym	Duchesse d'Istrie
Breeder	Laffay 1855
Blooms	Purple to lavender grey; large, double; summer-flowering; scent
Height and spread	6 × 6 ft (1.8 × 1.8 m)
Other uses	Climber

WILLIAM LOBB is sometimes catalogued as a climbing moss. A semi-rambling shrub, it will give color to the back of the border or to walls. It makes extremely vigorous growth with prickly stems and dark leaves.

CELESTE (ALBA)

Synonym	Celestial
Blooms	Very pale pink; semi-double, produced in clusters; summer-flowering; sweet scent
Height and spread	5 × 4 ft (1.5 × 1.2 m)
Other uses	Hedges; bush

CELESTE is a charming variety with its delicate combination of pale pink flowers and gray-green foliage. This outstanding border rose has an upright, bushy habit.

B A R O N   G I R O D   D E   L'A I N
(H Y B R I D   P E R P E T U A L)

Parentage	Sport of Eugene Furst 1897
Breeder	Reverchon 1897
Blooms	Crimson edged with silver; large, double, with a loose form, produced in small clusters; recurrent; moderate scent
Height and spread	4 × 3 ft (1.2 × 1 m)
Other uses	Cut flowers

BARON GIROD DE L'AIN has beautiful blooms that are pure Victoriana. It has dark leathery foliage on a rather straggly bush.

B O U L E   D E   N E I G E   (B O U R B O N)

Parentage	Blanche Lafitte × Sappho
Breeder	Lacharm 1867
Blooms	Pure white with a hint of pink in bud; small, double, round shape; recurrent; strong scent
Height and spread	4 × 3 ft (1.2 × 1 m)
Other uses	Cut flowers

BOULE DE NEIGE is a charming plant with pure white globe-shaped flowers. Give this rose extra feeding and it will bloom until late autumn. It produces coarse growth and has dark green glossy foliage.

C A M A I E U X   (G A L L I C A)

Breeder	Vibert 1830
Blooms	Pale pink striped with crimson-purple, turning to lavender and purple as they age; medium-sized, double; summer-flowering; sweet scent
Height and spread	30 × 30 in (75 × 75 cm)
Other uses	Cut flowers

CAMAIEUX is a tidy-looking plant with beautifully striped flowers. It responds to extra feeding and summer pruning. It has a short, shrubby habit and large, dark leathery leaves.

C A R D I N A L   D E   R I C H E L I E U   (G A L L I C A)

Breeder	Laffay 1840
Blooms	Deep purple; small to medium-sized, double; summer-flowering; sweet scent
Height and spread	3 × 3 ft (1 × 1 m)
Other uses	Bush

CARDINAL DE RICHELIEU is free-flowering, with relatively small flowers that are astonishing in their depth of color. It forms a compact, almost thornless shrub and has dark green leaves.

CHARLES DE MILLS (GALLICA)

Synonym	Bizarre Triomphant
Parentage	Origin unknown but probably before 1800
Blooms	Purple and deep red; very large, fully quartered, opening flat with a large number of petals: summer-flowering; strong scent
Height and spread	4 × 4 ft (1.2 × 1.2 m)
Other uses	Bush; cut flowers

CHARLES DE MILLS is an astonishing plant with huge blooms of extraordinary intricacy. An essential variety to grow in any collection of Old Garden Roses. It makes a bushy, but slightly lax plant with dark leathery leaves.

ROSA × CENTIFOLIA MUSCOSA (MOSS)

Synonyms	Common Moss; Old Pink Moss; Communis
Parentage	Discovered before 1700
Blooms	Rose pink; medium-sized, double; summer-flowering; strong scent
Height and spread	5 × 5 ft (1.5 × 1.5 m)
Other uses	Bush

ROSA × CENTIFOLIA MUSCOSA is the original old moss rose that was so common in cottage gardens. This rose gives a great show of color. It is a well-shaped shrub, with mossed stems and dark green leaves.

FANTIN-LATOUR (CENTIFOLIA)

Breeder	Discovered in the eighteenth century
Blooms	Delicate pink; medium-sized, cupped; summer-flowering; strong scent
Height and spread	7 × 7 ft (2 × 2 m)
Other uses	Semi-climber; cut flowers

FANTIN-LATOUR is very useful as an early summer shrub. It is a vigorous plant with glossy dark green leaves.

HONORINE DE BRABANT (BOURBON)

Blooms	Lilac-pink striped with red; large, double, quartered, produced in small clusters; moderate scent
Height and spread	6 × 6 ft (1.8 × 1.8 m)
Other uses	Cut flowers

HONORINE DE BRABANT has slightly cupped blooms with pronounced stripes and is an attractive, interesting shrub rose. It makes a vigorous, almost thornless, semi-sprawling bush with large, light green leaves.

KÖNIGIN VON DÄNEMARK *(ALBA)*

Synonym Queen of Denmark
Breeder Booth 1926
Blooms Deep to light pink; medium-sized, double, quartered; summer-flowering; strong scent
Height and spread 5 × 4 ft (1.5 × 1.2 m)
Other uses Bush

KÖNIGIN VON DÄNEMARK is the shortest of this group of old roses, but tremendously free-flowering. It is a robust plant which has gray-green foliage.

LOUISE ODIER *(BOURBON)*

Synonym Mme de Stella
Breeder Margottin 1851
Blooms Bright rose pink; large, double, camellia-shaped; recurrent; strong scent
Height and spread 6 × 4 ft (1.8 × 1.2 m)
Other uses Bush; cut flowers

LOUISE ODIER is a large plant. It has lax growth caused by the weight of bloom and may need support. The almost thornless stems are long and are useful in large floral arrangements. It has large, dark green leaves.

MADAME HARDY *(DAMASK)*

Breeder Hardy 1832
Blooms White with a green eye; large, double; summer-flowering; strong scent
Height and spread 5 × 4 ft (1.5 × 1.2 m)
Other uses Bush

MADAME HARDY when covered with flowers in mid-summer, is a fantastic sight. It makes a large, semi-rambling shrub with dark green foliage and requires very little maintenance.

NUITS DE YOUNG *(MOSS)*

Synonym Old Black
Breeder Laffay 1845
Blooms Velvety maroon to purple; small, double; summer-flowering; strong scent
Height and spread 4 × 3 ft (1.2 × 1 m)
Other uses Cut flowers

NUITS DE YOUNG is well worth growing for the depth of color in its beautifully shaped blooms. It has an upright habit with thin wiry stems and dark green leaves and responds to good feeding and no pruning.

PAUL NEYRON (HYBRID PERPETUAL)

Parentage Victor Verdier × Anna de
Diesbach
Breeder Levet 1869
Blooms Deep lilac-rose pink; very
large, double; recurrent; very
sweet scent
Height and spread 4 × 3 ft (1.2 × 1 m)
Other uses Cut flowers

PAUL NEYRON has very large blooms with the
sweetest of scents. The foliage is reminiscent of
modern Hybrid Teas. It makes a moderate-
sized bush with large, mid-green leaves.

REINE DES VIOLETTES (HYBRID PERPETUAL)

Synonym Queen of the Violets
Parentage Seedling of Pius IX
Breeder Millet-Malet 1860
Blooms Amethyst to purple; small to
medium-sized, very double;
recurrent; strong scent
Height and spread 4 × 3 ft (1.2 × 1 m)
Other uses Bush; cut flowers

REINE DES VIOLETTES is one of the smallest roses
in this category, but exquisitely beautiful with
its intricate flower form and fantastic scent. It is
a pretty shrub, slightly lax in growth, with dark
green leaves.

ROSA MUNDI (GALLICA)

Synonym *Rosa gallica* Versicolor
Parentage Sport of *Rosa gallica* var.
officinalis of ancient origin
Blooms Deep pink striped with blush
pink; large, semi-double,
produced in clusters;
summer-flowering; scent
Height and spread 3 × 3 ft (1 × 1 m)
Other uses Hedges

ROSA MUNDI is steeped in history, named after
Fair Rosamund, the mistress of the English
king Henry II. This superb short-growing
Gallica is very popular planted in groups and as
a hedge. Its mid-green foliage is subject to
mildew in the autumn. Occasionally this rose
loses its stripes and reverts to plain *officinalis*.

SOUVENIR DU DR JAMAIN (HYBRID PERPETUAL)

Parentage General Jacqueminot ×
Charles Lefebvre
Breeder Lacharme 1865
Blooms Velvety wine-red with
maroon shading; large,
double, cupped; recurrent;
strong scent
Height and spread 6 × 6 ft (1.8 × 1.8 m)
Other uses Semi-climber; cut flowers

SOUVENIR DU DR JAMAIN has tremendous depth
of color. It is a robust plant with dark leaves
and an arching habit. It has been a great
favorite as a cut flower, and can contribute to
a colorful border.

VARIEGATA DI BOLOGNA (BOURBON)

Breeder   Bonfiglioli 1909
Blooms   Creamy white, streaked and
stippled with crimson-purple;
medium-sized, double,
cupped, produced in small
clusters; recurrent; good scent
Height and spread   6 × 5 ft (1.8 × 1.5 m)
Other uses   Shrub

VARIEGATA DI BOLOGNA, when mature, is large and sprawling and covered in flowers. It has dull green foliage and may be prone to black spot in late summer.

WHITE MOSS (MOSS)

Synonyms   White Bath; Clifton Moss;
Shailer's White Moss
Parentage   Assumed to be a mutation of
Pink Moss
Breeder   Salter 1810
Blooms   Pure white; medium-sized,
double; summer-flowering;
good scent
Height and spread   4 × 4 ft (1.2 × 1.2 m)
Other uses   Shrub; cut flowers

WHITE MOSS has pure white flowers which give the impression of a blaze of light in a border. It makes a bushy plant with strong, well-mossed stems and dark green foliage.

HERMOSA (CHINA)

Synonyms   Armosa; Melanie Lemaire;
Mme Neumann
Breeder   Marcheseau 1840
Blooms   Clear pink; medium-sized,
semi-double; recurrent; very
little scent
Height and spread   3 × 2 ft (100 × 60 cm)
Other uses   Bush

HERMOSA is a short bushy plant for the front of the border which always seems to be in flower. It has grayish-green foliage and, if being used as a specimen bush, is best planted in clumps.

GREAT MAIDEN'S BLUSH (ALBA)

Synonyms   Cuisse de Nymphe; Emue;
Incarnata; Virginale
Breeder   Introduced before 1500
Blooms   Ivory and coral; medium-
sized, double, produced in
small clusters; summer-
flowering; good scent
Height and spread   7 × 5 ft (2 × 1.5 m)
Other uses   Shrub

GREAT MAIDEN'S BLUSH has healthy foliage of almost eucalyptus gray-green. It is an upright, vigorous plant and flowers for a long period in early summer.

FERDINAND PICHARD (HYBRID PERPETUAL)

Breeder Tanne 1921
Blooms Carmine striped and laced
white; large, globular,
produced in small clusters;
recurrent; good scent
Height and spread 5 × 4 ft (1.5 × 1.2 m)
Other uses Shrub; cut flowers

FERDINAND PICHARD, although a relative
newcomer, is probably the finest striped rose
and is one of the progenitors of some modern
striped roses. It is a shrubby grower with mid-
green, large leaves.

ROSA × ODORATA PALLIDA (CHINA)

Synonyms Old Blush China; Monthly
Rose; Parson's Pink
Parentage Unknown; introduced from
China in about 1752
Blooms Pink; medium, semi-double;
recurrent; little scent
Height and spread 1½ ft × 2 ft (75 × 60 cm)
Other uses Bush

ROSA × ODORATA PALLIDA was the variety which
introduced recurrent flowering, into the
European rose-breeding programs. It has a
very long flowering season, often continuing
well into the autumn. It is bushy with dull
green foliage.

ROGER LAMBELIN (HYBRID PERPETUAL)

Parentage Sport of Fisher Holmes
Breeder Schwartz
Blooms Dark red with a white rim to
the petals; medium, double,
produced in clusters;
recurrent; strong scent
Height and spread 4 × 2 ft (120 × 60 cm)
Other uses Cut flowers

ROGER LAMBELIN has a remarkably rich flower
colouring and its ruffled blooms are pure
Victoriana. Plentiful feeding and regular dead-
heading will be amply rewarded by an
outstanding display. This variety has an open
bushy habit and dark green foliage.

ROSA × CENTIFOLIA CRISTATA (CENTIFOLIA)

Synonyms Chapeau de Napoleon;
Crested Moss; Crested
Provence
Origin Introduced before 1827
Breeder Vibert 1827
Blooms Rose pink; double, produced
in clusters; summer-
flowering; strong scent
Height and spread 5 × 4 ft (1.5 × 1.2 m)
Other uses Shrub

ROSA × CENTIFOLIA is an intriguing rose. It has
large, very double flowers and buds that are
covered with green tufts or outgrowths, mossy
in appearance. The plant has a shrubby, rather
lax habit and foliage of an attractive deep green.

THE FORMAL ROSE GARDEN

Floribunda roses are the ideal choice

for a formal planting scheme.

The development of the Floribunda, the cluster-flowered bush rose, was a tremendous advance in contributing color to the garden. Many landscapers have discovered that planting Floribundas is more cost-effective than continually replanting bedding plants and certainly cheaper than maintaining lawns.

Well-maintained and healthy Floribundas will provide color from early summer to late autumn. Their color range is now as wide as that of the modern Hybrid Teas and their resistance to disease is being improved all the time. Their scent is also equal to some of the finest Hybrid Teas. Some Floribundas are a trifle too vigorous, but not the ones selected here. All of them require seasonal pruning, but it is simple to do. Reduce the growth by about two-thirds in the spring and dead-head well after the first flush of blooms to extend the flowering period.

Large swathes of color can be achieved with Floribundas. Although beds of a single variety look extremely impressive in a large area, in a limited space it is better to plant a mixture. Two compatible or complementary colors will give a stunning display; and added interest can be achieved by using standards of one or both varieties to give height. Another idea, particularly suitable for round beds, is to plant varieties in concentric circles, using a short variety on the outside and a taller one in the middle.

To give color early in the year, before the flowering season, plant bulbs among the roses. However, take care as the roses are dependent on the quality of sunlight they receive at the beginning of the growing season when they are endeavoring to make fresh growth. If the flowerheads are heavily underplanted with tulips, for instance, it can be disastrous, as they cut out light and put the roses at a disadvantage which they will have difficulty in overcoming later in the season.

There is also the matter of access at pruning time; and it can be very difficult to apply a heavy mulch of organic manure if the roses are surrounded by other plants. The answer is to be selective when planting your spring bulbs. Choose daffodils, for instance, and set them in tight groups well away from the roses.

As in all rose cultivation, attention to feeding is important to get the best results. Pests are not too much of a problem, but a seasonal spray against aphids is mandatory.

Many modern bush roses, such as Floribundas, give an excellent display when planted en masse. They fit very well into a formal garden and are much easier to maintain than bedding plants.

PRINCESS MICHAEL OF KENT (FLORIBUNDA)

Synonym Harlightly
Parentage Manx Queen × Alexander
Breeder Harkness 1981
Awards CM 1979
Blooms Pure medium yellow; large, double, produced in clusters; recurrent; scent
Height and spread 2 × 2 ft (60 × 60 cm)
Other uses Cut flowers

PRINCESS MICHAEL OF KENT has blooms which are rather big for the conventional Floribunda but the plant is very tough and will grow in quite poor soils. It is bushy and upright with glossy leaves.

BROWN VELVET (FLORIBUNDA)

Synonym Maccultra; Colourbreak
Parentage Mary Sumner × Kapai
Breeder McGredy 1983
Award GM New Zealand 1979
Blooms Russet; large, flat, produced in small clusters; recurrent; little scent
Height and spread 3 × 2 ft (90 × 60 cm)
Other uses Cut flowers

BROWN VELVET has large flat blooms which, with their beautiful quartered centers, are reminiscent of damask roses. The plant has a bushy habit and very dark foliage. It is lovely for flower arrangements.

THE TIMES ROSE (FLORIBUNDA)

Synonym Korpeahn; Carl Philip
Parentage Tornado × Redgold
Breeder Kordes 1984
Awards PIT 1982; Golden Rose of the Hague 1990
Blooms Bright crimson; medium to large, double, produced in clusters; recurrent; light scent
Height and spread 2½ × 2 ft (75 × 60 cm)
Other uses Standards

THE TIMES ROSE is absolutely stunning with its bright crimson flowers combined with dark, bronze-green foliage. It is probably the most disease-resistant rose ever introduced.

BETTY PRIOR (FLORIBUNDA)

Breeder Prior 1935
Awards GM 1933
Blooms Carmine pink with a white eye; medium-sized, single, produced in large clusters; recurrent; no scent
Height and spread 3 × 1½ ft (90 × 45 cm)
Other uses Borders

BETTY PRIOR is an old variety which is still popular. It has an upright habit and dark foliage.

ENGLISH MISS (*FLORIBUNDA*)

Parentage	Dearest × Sweet Repose
Breeder	Cant 1978
Awards	TGC 1977; BARB 1978
Blooms	Pale rosy blush; medium-sized, double; recurrent; strong scent
Height and spread	2½ × 2 ft (75 × 60 cm)
Other uses	Cut flowers

ENGLISH MISS has exquisite pink flowers which are subtly shaded. The growth is upright and the dark foliage sets off the blooms to perfection. This rose is a favorite for decorating the dinner table.

FRAGRANT DELIGHT (*FLORIBUNDA*)

Parentage	Chanelle × Whisky Mac
Breeder	Wisbech Plant Co. 1978
Awards	TGC 1976; Fragrance Medal 1976; JM 1988
Blooms	Light salmon tinged with orange; semi-double, large, produced in open clusters; recurrent; strong scent
Height and spread	3½ × 2½ ft (110 × 75 cm)
Other uses	Cut flowers

FRAGRANT DELIGHT is a valuable rose – tremendously free-flowering and with an appealing scent. It has an upright habit and glossy foliage with a reddish tinge.

HARVEST FAYRE (*FLORIBUNDA*)

Synonym	Dicnorth
Parentage	Seedling × Bright Smile
Breeder	Dickson 1990
Award	ROTY 1990
Blooms	Very bright orange apricot; medium-sized, double, produced in clusters; recurrent; light scent
Height and spread	2½ × 2 ft (75 × 60 cm)
Other uses	Cut flowers; standards

HARVEST FAYRE makes an eye-catching display when it is planted *en masse* in a bed. The heavy flower clusters stand up well to rain. It has an upright habit, light green leaves and is disease-resistant. Dead-head regularly to maintain continuous flowering.

MASQUERADE (*FLORIBUNDA*)

Parentage	Goldilocks × Holiday
Breeder	Boerner 1949
Awards	GM 1952
Blooms	Yellow turning to pink and red; small to medium, semi-double, produced in clusters; recurrent; little scent
Height and spread	3 × 2 ft (90 × 60 cm)
Other uses	Standards

MASQUERADE is a very free-flowering Floribunda which must be regularly and meticulously dead-headed to maintain a continuous show of flowers. The flowers change color as they age to provide a spectacular, multi-colored display. Masquerade has a bushy habit and dark green glossy foliage.

EUROPEANA (*FLORIBUNDA*)

Parentage	Ruth Leuwerik × Rosemary Rose
Breeder	De Ruiter 1963
Awards	GM The Hague 1962; CM 1963; AARS 1968
Blooms	Dark red; medium-sized, double, produced in large clusters; recurrent; scent
Height and spread	2½ × 1¾ ft (75 × 50 cm)
Other uses	Standards; exhibition

EUROPEANA has large, slightly drooping blooms of an almost red-currant hue complemented by dark leaves. The unusual coloring of this rose makes it a tremendous asset for any planting scheme. It is occasionally prone to mildew.

KORRESIA (*FLORIBUNDA*)

Synonyms	Friesia; Sunsprite
Parentage	Friedrich Worlein × Spanish Sun
Breeder	Kordes 1974
Award	GM Baden Baden 1972
Blooms	Clear bright yellow; medium-sized, produced in small clusters; recurrent; good scent
Height and spread	2½ × 2 ft (75 × 60 cm)
Other uses	Standards

KORRESIA was the first reliable yellow Floribunda to be introduced. It is a bushy, upright plant and is widely grown. The excellent scent is an added attraction.

CHRISTOPHER COLUMBUS (*FLORIBUNDA*)

Synonym	Poulstripe
Breeder	Poulsen 1992
Blooms	Pink striped cerise; medium-sized, semi-double, produced in clusters; recurrent; light scent
Height and spread	2 × 1½ ft (60 × 45 cm)
Other uses	Cut flowers

CHRISTOPHER COLUMBUS is a short Floribunda with a profusion of striped blooms which are dazzling in a rose bed. It is a bushy plant with medium-sized leaves.

ICEBERG (*FLORIBUNDA*)

Synonyms	Fée des Neiges; Schneewittchen; Korbin
Parentage	Robin Hood × Virgo
Breeder	Kordes 1958
Awards	GM, GM Baden Baden 1958;
Blooms	White; medium-sized, produced in clusters; recurrent; light scent
Height and spread	2½ × 2 ft (75 × 60 cm)
Other uses	Shrub; standards

ICEBERG is probably one of the greatest roses ever introduced. It is extremely vigorous and its production of flower throughout the summer is legendary. The beautiful blooms become tinged with pink in hot weather and are set off by the glossy, light green foliage. It can be prone to mildew in the autumn. This plant does not take kindly to hard pruning and is sometimes grown very successfully as a shrub.

MARGARET MERRIL (FLORIBUNDA)

Synonym   Harkuly
Parentage   (Rudolph Timm x Dedication) × Pascali
Breeder   Harkness 1977
Awards   CM 1978; Fragrance 1978; JM 1990
Blooms   Blush white; large, double, produced in small clusters; recurrent; strong scent
Height and spread   2½ × 2 ft (75 × 60 cm)
Other uses   Standards

MARGARET MERRIL has showy blooms, large for a Floribunda, which have a wonderful scent. It is a bushy plant with dark foliage.

ANISLEY DICKSON (FLORIBUNDA)

Synonyms   Dickimono, Dicky
Parentage   Coventry Cathedral × Memento
Breeder   Dickson 1983
Award   PIT 1984
Blooms   Deep salmon; medium-sized, double, produced in clusters; recurrent; scent
Height and spread   3 × 2 ft (90 × 60 cm)
Other uses   Cut flowers

ANISLEY DICKSON is a disease-resistant Floribunda which has prolific, lightly scented flowers in large clusters. It has a bushy habit and plentiful dark foliage.

SHEILA'S PERFUME (FLORIBUNDA)

Synonym   Harsherry
Parentage   Peer Gynt ×{Daily Sketch × (P. McGredy × Prima Ballerina)}
Breeder   Sheridan 1985
Awards   TGC 1981; Fragrance 1981
Blooms   Red, yellow; large, double; recurrent; strong scent
Height and spread   2½ × 2 ft (75 x 60 cm)
Other uses   Standards

SHEILA'S PERFUME lives up to its name with an excellent scent which is the perfect complement to a prettily colored rose. It is a bushy plant with glossy, luxuriant foliage.

AMBER QUEEN (FLORIBUNDA)

Synonym   Haroony
Parentage   Southampton × Typhoon
Breeder   Harkness 1984
Awards   CM 1983; ROTY 1984; AARS 1988; Golden Rose of the Hague 1991
Blooms   Pure amber yellow; medium-sized, double, in clusters; recurrent; strong scent
Height and spread   2 × 2 ft (60 × 60 cm)
Other uses   Standards

AMBER QUEEN is a useful bedding rose, which, if lightly pruned, will grow to 4 ft (1.2 m). The clear amber yellow blooms arrive early in summer. It has a bushy habit and is disease-resistant.

ANNE HARKNESS (FLORIBUNDA)

Synonym	Harkaramel
Parentage	Bobby Dazzler × seedling
Breeder	Harkness 1980
Awards	TGC 1978; BARB 1980
Blooms	Apricot yellow; medium-sized, double, produced in clusters; recurrent; light scent
Height and spread	3 × 2 ft (90 × 60 cm)
Other uses	Hedges; cut flowers

ANNE HARKNESS is a vigorous plant with an upright habit. The well-shaped blooms are very good for cutting.

TRUMPETER (FLORIBUNDA)

Synonym	Mactru
Parentage	Satchmo × seedling
Breeder	McGredy 1977
Awards	TGC 1974; BARB 1978; JMMGM 1991
Blooms	Orange-red; medium-sized, double, produced in clusters; recurrent; very little scent
Height and spread	2 × 1½ ft (60 × 45 cm)
Other uses	Containers, window boxes

TRUMPETER is a very brilliant red and is ideal for small beds and pots. It is a short bushy plant with glossy foliage. The large clusters require frequent dead-heading to maintain flowering throughout the summer.

BUCK'S FIZZ (FLORIBUNDA)

Synonyms	Poulgan; Gavn
Parentage	Seedling × Mary Sumner
Breeder	Poulsen 1988
Award	TGC 1987
Blooms	Vibrant bright orange; medium-sized, double, produced in small clusters; recurrent; light scent
Height and spread	3½ × 2 ft (110 × 60 cm)
Other uses	Cut flowers

BUCK'S FIZZ is a vigorous rose with an upright habit. Plants of this rose will fill a bed well and provide bright color all summer.

MANY HAPPY RETURNS (FLORIBUNDA)

Synonyms	Harwanted; Prima
Parentage	Herbstfeuer × Pearl Drift
Breeder	Harkness 1991
Award	TGC 1990
Blooms	Pale blush pink; double, produced in clusters; recurrent; scent
Height and spread	3 × 3 ft (90 × 90 cm)
Other uses	Hedges; shrub; standards

MANY HAPPY RETURNS is a versatile plant which many gardeners are undecided whether to call a bush or a shrub. It has a very bushy habit and glossy foliage. When lightly pruned it will develop into a good specimen plant.

IN SPLENDID ISOLATION

Allow some of your bush roses to grow tall and shrubby; they will flower better and provide splendid focal points.

The pursuit of the perfect flower and the cultivation of the rose as a bedding plant have largely obscured the fact that, originally, most roses were shrubs growing about 6 ft (2 m) in height. In recent years it has been found, by chance, that many rose varieties grown as bushes, about 3–4 ft (1–1.2 m) tall, will improve if they are allowed to develop into shrubs. Not every variety responds to this method of culture, and those that grow naturally upright or are prone to disease should be avoided. However, it is a simple way of growing roses, including some Hybrid Teas and Floribundas (see pages 104–111 and 120–125).

Some of the best roses for growing in this way are the Rugosas; the "Frühlings" range of shrub roses can also give an outstanding display; and the white rose "Nevada" reigns supreme. Try planting your chosen variety in groups of three or five for maximum impact, in a lawn or informal area of the garden. You will be thrilled by the mass of color and natural, unfettered shape of the roses.

To grow roses as specimen shrubs do not prune them back hard. Lightly prune in the spring and allow them to develop progressively more wood until, after about four seasons, the plant has reached a height of about 4 ft (1.2 m). Throughout this time feed the rose well, applying a thick mulch of well-rotted manure together with a good dressing of rose fertilizer after the spring pruning. Continue to feed throughout the growing season, with a final application immediately after the first flush of flowers is over in mid-summer. The plants need little more attention apart from the control of aphids and other predators, and an application of systemic fungicide in mid-summer.

◀ *Many roses, when lightly pruned and well fed develop into very good shrubs. "Fritz Nobis" is a beautiful sight when grown in a lawn in this way, with flowers cascading down right to the grass.*

MOUNTBATTEN (*FLORIBUNDA*)

Synonym	Harmantelle
Parentage	Peer Gynt{(Anne Cocker × Arthur Bell) × Southampton}
Breeder	Harkness 1982
Awards	GM 1979: ROTY 1982
Blooms	Yellow; large, double; recurrent; scent
Height and spread	5 × 3 ft (1.5 × 1 m)
Other uses	Borders; cut flowers

MOUNTBATTEN is vigorous with an upright habit and plentiful flowers. It has glossy foliage and is very disease-resistant.

TANGO (*FLORIBUNDA*)

Synonyms	Macfirwal, Rock 'n Roll, Stretch Johnson
Parentage	Sexy Rexy × Maestro
Breeder	McGredy 1988
Awards	GM 1988; SM Glasgow 1990
Blooms	Orange-scarlet, rimmed with white, yellow center; medium to large, double, produced in clusters; recurrent; little scent
Height and spread	4 × 3 ft (1.2 × 1 m)
Other uses	Borders; standards

TANGO is catalogued as a bush in the UK, but it will grow to about 6 ft (1.8 m) and makes an excellent shrub. It has a bushy habit and the flowers are eye-catching.

MADAME PLANTIER (*ALBA NOISETTE*)

Synonym	*R. alba* Madame Plantier
Parentage	*R. alba* × *R. moschata* hybrid
Breeder	Plantier 1835
Blooms	Pure white; semi-double, medium-sized; produced in large clusters; summer-flowering; strong scent
Height and spread	8 × 12 ft (2.4 × 3.7 m)
Other uses	Borders

MADAME PLANTIER will form a large shrub when fully grown. The gently arching stems bear masses of flowers to give an outstanding summer display. This easy-going rose requires virtually no pruning.

SOUTHAMPTON (*FLORIBUNDA*)

Synonym	Susan Ann
Parentage	(Anne Elizabeth × Allgold) × Yellow Cushion
Breeder	Harkness 1971
Award	TGC 1971
Blooms	Apricot flushed with red; large, double, produced in clusters; recurrent; strong scent
Height and spread	4 × 3 ft (1.2 × 1 m)
Other uses	Borders; cut flowers

SOUTHAMPTON grows vigorously and has an upright habit. It is very free-flowering and the soft coloring of the blooms is enhanced by the luxuriant dark foliage.

FRÜHLINGSGOLD (MODERN SHRUB)

Synonym	Spring Gold
Parentage	Joanna Hill ×
	R. pimpinellifolia altaica
Breeder	Kordes 1941
Blooms	Primrose yellow; large, double or semi-double; early summer flowering; scent
Height and spread	10 × 4 ft (3 × 1.2 m)
Other uses	Borders

FRÜHLINGSGOLD is one of the "Frühlings" family of spectacular rose shrubs which can develop into very large plants. It is no exception and has a vigorous, arching habit. The foliage is light green, complementing the flowers well.

THE QUEEN ELIZABETH (FLORIBUNDA)

Parentage	Charlotte Armstrong × Floradora
Breeder	Lammerts 1954
Awards	PIT 1955
Blooms	Cyclamen pink; large, double, produced in clusters; recurrent; light scent
Height and spread	6 × 3 ft (1.8 × 1 m)
Other uses	Borders; cut flowers

THE QUEEN ELIZABETH is a tremendously popular rose whose vigor and prolific flowers are legendary. Prune every spring by about half to prevent it getting leggy.

ROYAL WILLIAM (HYBRID TEA)

Synonyms	Korzuan, Duftsauber 84, Fragrant Charm 84
Parentage	Feuerzauber × seedling
Breeder	Kordes 1984
Awards	TGC 1985; ROTY 1987
Blooms	Deep crimson red; large, double; recurrent; strong scent
Height and spread	3½ × 2½ ft (1.1 m × 75 cm)
Other uses	Beds; standards

ROYAL WILLIAM is the first heavily scented red Hybrid Tea that has good disease resistance. It is a robust, upright-growing plant with large leaves. When well fed and lightly pruned it develops into a shrub about 6 ft (1.8 m) tall.

NEVADA (MODERN SHRUB)

Parentage	La Giralda × *R. moyesii*
Breeder	Dot 1927
Blooms	Creamy white; large, semi-double; very early; recurrent; scent
Height and spread	9 × 5 ft (2.7 × 1.5 m)
Other uses	Borders

NEVADA is a spectacular plant with arching growth which should be allowed to grow naturally and never be cut back. When well fed it will produce some color in the autumn. The pink form is called Marguerite Hilling.

Cerise Bouquet (*Modern Shrub*)

Parentage R. multibracteata × Crimson Glory
Breeder Tantau 1958
Blooms Cherry red; medium-sized, double, produced in clusters; recurrent; light scent
Height and spread 12 × 12 ft (3.7 × 3.7 m)
Other uses Standards

Cerise Bouquet is a spectacular, very large plant. It has gray-green foliage and is free-flowering in the summer. It requires no attention and should be allowed enough space to grow freely.

Peace (*Hybrid Tea*)

Synonyms Gioia; Gloria Dei; Mme Meilland
Parentage Seedling × Margaret McGredy
Breeder Meilland 1942
Awards AARS 1946; GM 1947; Golden Rose of the Hague 1965
Blooms Yellow flushed with pink; large, double; recurrent; slight scent
Height and spread 4 × 3 ft (1.2 × 1 m)
Other uses Beds; standards; exhibition

Peace is probably the most famous rose ever introduced. Bred in the south of France, it gained world-wide recognition at the inauguration of the United Nations in San Francisco in 1945. It is a robust plant with large dark leaves.

Fritz Nobis (*Modern Shrub*)

Parentage Joanna Hill × Magnifica
Breeder Kordes 1940
Blooms Light rose tinged with salmon pink; medium-sized, double, produced in clusters; summer-flowering; scent
Height and spread 10 × 5 ft (3 × 1.5 m)
Other uses Borders

Fritz Nobis is a plant that will develop naturally into a very good shrub. It grows vigorously and has dense, gray-green foliage. The beautiful flowers cover the bush.

Scabrosa (*Rugosa*)

Synonym R. rugosa Scabrosa
Breeder Introduced by Harkness 1950
Blooms Reddish mauve; large, single; recurrent; good scent
Height and spread 5 × 5 ft (1.5 × 1.5 m)
Other uses Hedges

Scabrosa is the densest growing of any of the Rugosa varieties and provides excellent cover for birds and other wildlife. This is an exceptional rose, which grows vigorously and has a robust constitution. It produces large leaves, large flowers and clusters of huge, round, red hips in autumn.

A CARPET OF ROSES

Ground-cover roses are the perfect choice for brightening up some of the most difficult and unpromising places in the garden.

The latest breed of easy-care, ground-cover roses was originally developed for municipal purposes: to beautify housing projects and highway landscaping and to enhance inner-city planting schemes. In seeking to satisfy the ideals of town planners and developers, rose-breeders created a new group of colorful, spreading, relatively disease-free roses, requiring the minimum of attention. Not only have these ground-cover roses proved their worth in public places, but they now also make a great contribution to private gardens.

They provide an ideal covering for steep banks and neglected areas of the garden where little but weeds seem to grow. Ground-cover roses are also perfect for town gardens, where the air quality may be poor. Their ability to flourish along major highways means that traffic pollution is not the problem it is for many other groups of favorite plants. Some of the smaller varieties make excellent specimens and can be used on patios and in containers and window boxes.

Originally two distinct types of ground-cover roses were developed. The first type had a horizontal-spreading habit. These ranged from miniatures, which grow only as high as 9 in (23 cm), but spread 3–4 ft (1–1.2 m), up to grander plants of 2 ft (60 cm), spreading 12–15 ft (3.7–4.6 m). The second type has a mushroom-like form, reaching heights of 3–5 ft (1–1.5 m) and spreading 6–8 ft (1.8–2.4 m). However, more recent developments are blurring the boundaries between these two groups.

Like all roses, ground covers need a good start. Remove all weeds from the site and dig in a generous amount of organic material before planting. However, once these roses are established and growing strongly, their demands are minimal. As well as suppressing weeds, the dense spreading growth needs little pruning.

Large and small varieties of modern ground-cover roses will clothe the most inhospitable areas of the garden and flower from mid-summer to late autumn.

SMARTY (GROUND COVER)

Synonym Intersmart
Parentage Yesterday × seedling
Breeder Interplant 1979
Blooms Deep pink; large, single, produced in clusters; recurrent; light scent
Height and spread 3 × 5 ft (1 × 1.5 m)
Other uses Borders; landscaping

SMARTY has made a valuable contribution to municipal planting schemes and has proved to be a very reliable plant in gardens also. It is bushy with dark foliage.

SNOW CARPET (GROUND COVER)

Synonyms Maccarpe; Blanche Neige; Schneeteppich
Parentage New Penny × Temple Bells
Breeder McGredy 1980
Award TGC 1978
Blooms Creamy white; very small, double, produced in clusters; recurrent; little scent
Height and spread 1 × 4 ft (30 × 120 cm)
Other uses Containers and window boxes; standards

SNOW CARPET will grow in the most difficult situations and strikes easily from cuttings. It is a low-growing, spreading plant with small leaves.

GWENT (GROUND COVER)

Synonym Poulurt
Breeder Poulsen 1992
Blooms Bright yellow; double, small- to medium-sized, produced in clusters; recurrent; strong scent
Height and spread 1½ × 3 ft (45 × 90 cm)
Other uses Containers and window boxes; standards

GWENT is a welcome addition to these increasingly popular plants. Spectacular when planted on banks in quantity, it is a sprawling plant with dark, glossy foliage.

BONICA (GROUND COVER)

Synonyms Meidomonac; Demon
Parentage (*R. sempervirens* × Mlle Marthe Carron) × Picasso
Breeder Meilland 1981
Awards CM Belfast 1982; ADR 1983; AARS 1987
Blooms Pink; medium, double, in clusters; little scent
Height and spread 4 × 4 ft (1.2 × 1.2 m)
Other uses Hedges; landscaping

BONICA is a variety which has caught the imagination of landscapers in the USA. It is vigorous with lax growth. There are sometimes repeat flowers in the autumn.

R E D   M A X   G R A F   (GROUND COVER)

Synonyms   Kormax; Rote Max Graf
Parentage   R. kordesii × seedling
Breeder   Kordes 1980
Award   GM Baden Baden 1979
Blooms   Bright crimson red; very large, single, produced in clusters; summer-flowering; light scent
Height and spread   1.2 × 6 m (4 × 20 ft)
Other uses   Landscaping

RED MAX GRAF will easily cover large banks and terraces. It is a very sprawling plant with plentiful foliage and single blooms which are quite dramatic in their effect.

G R O U S E   (GROUND COVER)

Synonyms   Korimro; Immensee; LacRose
Parentage   The Fairy × R. wichuraiana
Breeder   Kordes 1984
Blooms   Blush pink; small, semi-double; summer-flowering; strong scent
Height and spread   60 cm × 3 m (2 × 10 ft)
Other uses   Landscaping

GROUSE is low-growing and spreads to cover a large area. The pale flowers are attractive against their background of small, glossy leaves. This is a hardy and disease-resistant plant, which should not be pruned.

M A G I C   C A R P E T   (GROUND COVER)

Synonym   Jaclover
Breeder   Zary/Warriner 1992
Award   ROTY 1996
Blooms   Lavender; small to medium-sized, produced in clusters; recurrent; spicy scent
Height and spread   45 × 120 cm (1½ × 4 ft)
Other uses   Standards

MAGIC CARPET is a rose which has rapidly become popular around the world. The light green foliage adds to the beauty of a spreading plant which requires virtually no pruning.

F E R D Y   (GROUND COVER)

Synonyms   Keitoli; Ferdi
Parentage   Climbing seedling × Petit Folie seedling
Breeder   Suzuki 1984
Blooms   Fuchsia pink; small, double, produced in large clusters; recurrent; no scent
Height and spread   1 × 1.2 m (3 × 4 ft)
Other uses   Borders; landscaping

FERDY is a very popular variety that is remarkably disease-resistant. A vigorous plant with dense foliage. The flower stems are spiky and the small leaves are dainty. It may need staking before it becomes established.

RED BLANKET (GROUND COVER)

Synonym	Intercell
Parentage	Yesterday × seedling
Breeder	Ilsink 1979
Blooms	Rosy red, pale on the inside; medium-sized, semi-double, produced in clusters; recurrent; light scent
Height and spread	75 × 180 cm (2½ × 12 ft)
Other uses	Borders; landscaping

RED BLANKET is a widely grown, reliable rose which is used extensively in urban planting schemes. Disease-resistant and free flowering, it is a bushy, spreading plant with dark, almost evergreen foliage.

PINK BELLS (GROUND COVER)

Synonym	Poulbells
Parentage	Mini-Poul × Temple Bells
Breeder	Poulsen 1983
Blooms	Bright pink; small, double, produced in large clusters; summer-flowering; little scent
Height and spread	75 × 150 cm (2½ × 5 ft)
Other uses	Landscaping

PINK BELLS has a fantastic show of high-quality flowers for about four weeks in mid-summer. It is a large, spreading plant with glossy leaves.

PEARL MEIDILAND (GROUND COVER)

Synonyms	Meiplaten; Perle Meillandécor
Breeder	Meilland 1979
Blooms	Pale pearl pink; medium-sized, semi-double, produced in clusters; recurrent; good scent
Height and spread	60 × 150 cm (2 × 5 ft)
Other uses	Standards

PEARL MEIDILAND is a vigorous plant which is extremely disease-resistant. The plant has small green leaves and is very hardy.

SCARLET MEIDILAND (GROUND COVER)

Synonyms	Meikrotal; Scarlet Meillandécor
Breeder	Meilland 1987
Award	CM Glasgow 1990
Blooms	Vivid scarlet; small, double, produced in clusters; recurrent; little scent
Height and spread	90 × 180 cm (3 × 6 ft)
Other uses	Standards

SCARLET MEIDILAND is an outstanding plant with huge sprays of flowers and small, glossy leaves. Dead-head regularly to maintain flowering into the autumn.

RAISED BEDS AND ROCK GARDENS

*Ground-cover roses make a marvellous sight
when grown at varying levels.*

Low walls, raised beds and rock gardens offer exciting opportunities for introducing roses into the garden. Ground-cover roses are grown very successfully in these situations. By making use of the different levels you can display them very well – this is a popular device often employed by garden designers. Roses with a spreading or relaxed habit are particularly suitable as they will tumble over low walls and raised beds, providing the soil is sufficiently rich and deep.

Low walls with an integral hollow planting space should be built about 18 in (45 cm) wide in order to accommodate the root systems of prostrate and spreading roses. Most of the recurrent ground-cover varieties are suitable; my favorite choice is "Suffolk" (see page 135). Some of the older ramblers (see pages 78–85) are good, too, but remember that many of these are not repeat-flowering.

Raised beds give the opportunity for many interesting schemes as well as being convenient for elderly or handicapped gardeners. A particularly successful arrangement is a series of square raised beds, 6 × 6 × 2–3 ft (180 × 180 × 60–90 cm), constructed at different levels, preferably in stone. A stunning pyramid effect is achieved by planting a short-stemmed standard in the center of each bed and surrounding it with a ground-cover rose of the same variety.

A few miniature roses are even suitable for the rock garden, but they will only be successful if they are planted in deep pockets of specially prepared soil. Their success depends upon your using a good strong potting compost, such as John Innes No. 3, or a home-made mixture of equal parts good loam, well-rotted manure and peat or peat substitute. Once the plants are established, apply a rose fertilizer in spring and early summer, and water whenever the soil shows signs of drying out.

Choose varieties such as "Snow Carpet" (see page 131) and pale pink "Nozomi" (see page 135) which both have the small leaves and flowers that are appropriate for raised beds and rock gardens. Many of the more exotically colored miniatures and patio roses have a more upright habit which is not suitable for spreading over low walls or softening the edges of raised beds.

*The pink rose, "Raubritter," cascades over a low wall above
a clump of* Alchemilla mollis *to make a striking display.*

FLOWER CARPET (GROUND COVER)

Synonyms	Blooming Carpet; Emera; Heidetraum; Noatraum
Parentage	Immensee × Amanda
Breeder	Noack 1991
Awards	1990, TGC, ADR; 1991, GM The Hague, GM Dortmund
Blooms	Deep pink; small to medium, semi-double, produced in clusters; recurrent; little scent
Height and spread	1½ × 3 ft (45 × 90 cm)
Other uses	Containers and window boxes

FLOWER CARPET, with its display of flowers over a long period and enviable health record, is proving to be an extremely popular variety. It forms a spreading bush, covered with small dark green leaves.

NOZOMI (GROUND COVER)

Synonym	Heiderröslein
Parentage	Fairy Princess × Sweet Fairy
Breeder	Onodera 1968
Blooms	Blush pink; very small, single, produced in large clusters; summer-flowering; little scent
Height and spread	1 × 6 ft (30 cm × 1.8 m)
Other uses	Standards; banks

NOZOMI flowers prolifically and has very small green leaves. It is grown all over the world and used successfully in many situations, including small gardens, landscapes and steep banks.

SEA FOAM (GROUND COVER)

Parentage	Seedling of The Fairy
Breeder	Schwartz 1964
Award	GM Rome 1966
Blooms	Pure white; small to medium-sized, double, produced in large clusters; recurrent; scent
Height and spread	1 × 3 ft (30 × 90 cm)
Other uses	Standards; small spaces

SEA FOAM has a sprawling habit and dark green, glossy foliage. Its magnificent display of flowers over a long period makes a great contribution to any garden. It is disease-resistant.

SUFFOLK (GROUND COVER)

Synonyms	Kormixal; Bassino
Parentage	(Sea Foam × Red Max Graf) × seedling
Breeder	Kordes 1988
Award	TGC 1990
Blooms	Crimson scarlet with prominent yellow stamens; small, single, produced in clusters; recurrent; scent
Height and spread	1 × 3 ft (30 × 90 cm)
Other uses	Standards; small spaces

SUFFOLK has small, dark green leaves and forms a low, spreading shrub. It is a free-flowering, disease-resistant rose. In autumn it produces an eye-catching display of small orange-red hips. Because of its small neat form it is ideal for small-scale plantings.

SURREY (GROUND COVER)

Synonyms	Korlanum; Vent d'Eté
Parentage	The Fairy × seedling
Breeder	Kordes 1988
Award	GM 1987
Blooms	Soft pink with a deeper pink eye; medium-sized, double, produced in large clusters; recurrent; scent
Height and spread	2½ × 4 ft (75 × 120 cm)
Other uses	Borders, standards

SURREY is a very free-flowering rose with a relaxed, shrubby habit. The lovely blooms become frilly as they age.

WHITE FLOWER CARPET (GROUND COVER)

Synonym	Schneeflocke
Parentage	Grouse × Margaret Merril
Breeder	Noack 1993
Award	GM 1991
Blooms	Pure white; large, semi-double, produced in clusters; recurrent; scent
Height and spread	2½ ×4 ft (75 × 120 cm)
Other uses	Borders; standards

WHITE FLOWER CARPET is one of the most hardy of ground-cover roses, being both disease- and weather-resistant. It is free-flowering with very dark foliage.

CHILTERNS (GROUND COVER)

Synonyms	Kortemma; Fiery Sunsation; Mainaufeur; Red Ribbons
Breeder	Kordes 1990
Blooms	Deep crimson; semi-double, small to medium-sized, produced in clusters; recurrent; little scent
Height and spread	1½ × 9 ft (75 cm × 3 m)
Other uses	Standards

CHILTERN is a free-flowering, adaptable variety which can be used in many situations in the garden. The bright green leaves are a perfect foil for the stunning flowers.

PARTRIDGE (GROUND COVER)

Synonyms	Korweirim; Lac Blanc; Weisse Immense
Parentage	The Fairy × seedling
Breeder	Kordes 1982
Awards	CM 1984
Blooms	White; small, semi-double, produced in clusters, summer-flowering; strong scent
Height and spread	1½ × 12 ft (45 cm × 4 m)
Other uses	Landscaping

PARTRIDGE grows rampantly and is ideal for covering large areas. It is hardy and extremely disease-resistant. The flowers are most attractive set against the small dark leaves.

SWANY (GROUND COVER)

Synonym Meiburenac
Parentage R. sempervirens × Mlle Carron
Breeder Meilland 1978
Blooms White; medium-sized, double, produced in clusters; recurrent; little scent
Height and spread 2 × 3 ft (60 × 90 cm)
Other uses Containers and window boxes; standards

SWANY has blooms which are larger than most ground-cover roses, so when planting allow enough space around the plant to display them well. It is a bushy plant with a lax habit and dark glossy foliage.

SUMA (GROUND COVER)

Synonym Harsuma
Parentage Seedling of Nozomi
Breeder Onodera 1989
Blooms Ruby-red fading to deep pink; small, produced in large clusters; summer-flowering; no scent
Height and spread 1½ × 3 ft (45 × 150 cm)
Other uses Standards

SUMA is an adaptable plant which has been described as a red Nozomi. It has a long flowering period and the small dark leaves turn to bronze-green in the autumn.

ALBA MEIDILAND (GROUND COVER)

Synonym Meiflopin; Alba Meillandécor; Alba Sunglaze
Breeder Meilland 1989
Blooms White; medium-sized, double, produced in large clusters; recurrent; little scent
Height and spread 2 × 4 ft (60 × 120 cm)
Other uses Landscaping and standards

ALBA MEIDILAND is a dense-growing, lax plant with small dark green leaves. It is a very disease-resistant variety.

ESSEX (GROUND COVER)

Synonyms Poulnoz; Pink Cover
Parentage The Fairy × seedling
Breeder Poulsen 1989
Awards CM 1987; GM Dublin 1988
Blooms Reddish pink with a white center; small, single, produced in large clusters; recurrent; little scent
Height and spread 2 × 4 ft (60 × 120 cm)
Other uses Small borders; containers and window boxes; standards

ESSEX produces masses of flowers, and regular dead-heading will ensure a continuous display. It is a neat, semi-sprawling plant with small dark leaves.

HAPPY MARRIAGES

Roses combine very well with other plants, many of which will provide color after the roses have flowered.

Roses make eye-catching features, but must also work as an integral part of the whole garden. Almost all of them can be "happily married" to other colorful fragrant plants which will take over when the roses are not in bloom. There is a wide range of compatible partners to choose from.

For example, the rambling and climbing roses which only bloom once in the summer will happily play host to the spring-flowering *Clematis montana* and *C. montana* var. *rubens* and, for late-summer flowers, to *C. × jackmanii*, and its cultivars, which can be pruned at the same time as the host plant. Honeysuckle, such as the woodbine, *Lonicera periclymenum*, will also add flowers and late-evening fragrance to the planting.

Dwarf lavender (*Lavandula angustifolia* "Munstead" or "Hidcote") is a traditional, colorful and sweet-smelling edging for rose beds, or for a more formal appearance, use box (*Buxus sempervirens* "Suffruticosa"). However, box has an invasive root system and you should allow plenty of space between it and the roses.

Bright, interesting shrubs are a great bonus, particularly in the winter and early spring. The various forms of *Elaeagnus* are excellent combined with roses. These bushes, with their attractive, often variegated foliage and, in many cases, very fragrant flowers, are a tremendous asset to the garden, and a refreshing change to the ubiquitous dull evergreens.

In middle to late spring, daffodils and dwarf iris bring color and leaf interest. However, care has to be taken when planting bulbs because young roses need as much light as possible, particularly in early spring, and the foliage of tall-growing daffodils can obscure this. Also, it is very important to leave space around the base of roses for mulches and fertilizers.

Once they have had their moment of glory, groups of Old Garden Roses can be brightened by underplantings of dwarf and low-growing bedding dahlias, many of which have interesting foliage. There are also the low-growing, very free-flowering pinks (*Dianthus*) which have a wide color range and the added advantage of being excellent cut flowers. All roses combine very well with gray foliage plants. The bright color of some modern roses, for example, is set off well by the gray leaves of *Senecio cineraria*, *Artemisia* "Silver Queen" and *Stachys byzantina*.

◀ *An attractive planting plan for a raised bed combines a dark red ground-cover rose with silvery artemisia backed by an ornamental maple.*

▶ *Traditional borders filled with shrub roses and herbaceous plants spill over a grass path. The plant colors complement the roses beautifully.*

◀ *The Hybrid Musk "Penelope" fits beautifully into a mixed planting plan,* which includes blue delphiniums and Geranium himalayense *"Irish Blue."*

◀ *The perfect pink of the shrub rose "Fritz Nobis" teamed with a purple-leafed berberis is a very pleasing color combination.*

▶ *The rose growing over the trellis in the center is just beginning to go over, but the other plants, including the lavender hedge in the foreground, will provide continued interest.*

ROSES AS CUT FLOWERS

The fascinating colors and textures of roses make them marvellous flowers for arranging in a vase.

Whether bunched casually in a favorite vase or as part of a carefully arranged formal display, there are few flowers more favored for cutting than roses. It is the ideal way in which to appreciate the form and colors of special roses at close quarters.

Guests of the Roman emperor Heliogabalus are said to have been suffocated by the weight of rose petals strewn at his lavish banquets! Roses are used less extravagantly today, but continue to be associated with special occasions, as proved by their use in bouquets, floral tributes and flower arrangements.

Cut roses must take up water and last well. Not all garden roses fulfil these criteria and collapse immediately they are cut. Many of the "hand-painted" Floribundas, such as "Matangi" (see page 147), are disappointing in this way. White and pink roses seem to have a longer vase life than red or bicolored blooms. Long stems are always preferable to short ones. For this reason Bourbon roses, such as "La Reine Victoria," make ideal cut flowers whereas other Old Garden Roses, which flower on two-year-old wood, will not take up

water to any great extent and start to shed their petals after about a day.

Gather roses in the early morning or late in the evening, but never in the heat of the day. Ideally, cut them the day before they are needed to allow time for "conditioning." This means, immediately after cutting, plunging them up to their necks in a bucket of cold water to which has been added a cut-flower preserver (or tablespoon of sugar or glucose). The preserver not only helps the stems to draw up water, but also keeps the water fresh as it kills harmful bacteria. Place the bucket of flowers in a cool dark place, preferably overnight.

Florists' foam gives stability to an arrangement and also prolongs the life of the blooms. Before the flowers are inserted the foam must be thoroughly soaked in water containing cut-flower preserver. Before arranging your roses remove the thorns and lower leaves. Also cut off at least 1/2 in (1 cm) of each stem; this gets rid of any air pockets which would impede the uptake of water. Even if you are not using florists' foam, prepare the roses as described.

◄ *Roses arranged informally with their leaves in a shallow glass dish would make an attractive centerpiece for a mid-summer dinner party.*

► *Florists' foam has not been used in this simple arrangement of pink and cream roses. Pale roses like these last longer than some of the deeper colors.*

ALEXANDER *(HYBRID TEA)*

Synonym	Alexandra
Parentage	Super Star × (Ann Elizabeth × Allgold)
Breeder	Harkness 1972
Award	CM 1972
Blooms	Bright vermilion; large, double; petals sometimes scalloped as they open; recurrent; light scent
Height and spread	6 × 3 ft (1.8 × 1 m)
Other uses	Bush

ALEXANDER has shiny foliage and grows very vigorously. It should be pruned lightly so that its natural upright form can fully develop. The blooms have very long stems making this an ideal rose for cutting.

CONGRATULATIONS *(HYBRID TEA)*

Synonyms	Korlift; Sylvia
Parentage	Carina × seedling
Breeder	Kordes 1978
Awards	BARB 1978
Blooms	Rose pink; long, pointed, double, produced in small clusters; recurrent; good scent
Height and spread	5 × 3 ft (1.5 × 1 m)
Other uses	Borders; bush

CONGRATULATIONS is a fast-growing rose with dark green foliage. Although it produces a good display of flowers, vigorous disbudding is recommended in order to achieve top-quality blooms of perfect form. The flowers last well in water.

FELLOWSHIP *(HYBRID TEA)*

Synonym	Harwelcome
Parentage	Southampton × Remember Me
Breeder	Harkness 1992
Award	GM 1990
Blooms	Deep orange; medium-sized, double, produced in small clusters; recurrent; good scent
Height and spread	3 × 2 ft (90 × 60 cm)
Other uses	Bedding; borders

FELLOWSHIP develops a bushy habit with glossy, dark green foliage. It is a hardy free-flowering rose. The long stems, in combination with its classically shaped blooms and rich color, make this a favorite rose among flower arrangers.

LOVING MEMORY *(HYBRID TEA)*

Synonyms	Korgund; Burgundy 81
Parentage	Seedling × Red Planet
Breeder	Kordes 1981
Award	TGC 1982
Blooms	Dark red; well-shaped, very large; recurrent; light scent
Height and spread	3½ × 2 ft (110 × 60 cm)
Other uses	Bedding; specimen; standards

LOVING MEMORY is an excellent source of cut flowers due to its prodigious production of high-quality blooms. The leaves are large and dark green, a good foil for the flowers.

MADAME ISAAC PEREIRE (BOURBON)

Breeder Garçon 1881
Blooms Very deep pink to purple;
very large, double; recurrent;
very heavy scent
Height and spread 6 × 5 ft (1.8 × 1.5 m)
Other uses Walls; borders; bush

MADAME ISAAC PEREIRE is well worth growing just for its scent. However, it also produces a huge number of flowers throughout summer. It is a vigorous plant with large leaves. It is suitable for growing against a wall, as in more open situations it may require support.

LA REINE VICTORIA (BOURBON)

Synonyms The Shell Rose
Parentage Seedling of Pius IX 1860
Breeder Millet-Malet 1860
Blooms Rich pink which darkens as
the flowers age; large,
rounded, recurrent; very good
scent
Height and spread 6 × 5 ft (1.8 × 1.5 m)
Other uses Borders; bush

LA REINE VICTORIA is a perfect rose for cut-flower arrangements due to its long stems and large rounded blooms, so typical of a Bourbon rose. In the border it makes a large, handsome, sprawling shrub with arching stems.

SELFRIDGES (HYBRID TEA)

Synonyms Korpriwa; Berolina
Breeder Kordes 1984
Award ADR 1986
Blooms Bright yellow; large, with
long, pointed buds, borne
singly; recurrent; good scent
Height and spread 4 × 2½ ft (120 × 75 cm)
Other uses Bedding; specimen; for
exhibition

SELFRIDGES develops into a very decorative specimen plant with vigorous growth and dark green foliage. It produces a large number of perfectly formed flowers on long straight stems. These attributes make it a good rose for showing and for cut-flower arrangements.

SEXY REXY (FLORIBUNDA)

Synonyms Macrexy; Heckenzauber
Parentage Seaspray × Dreaming
Breeder McGredy 1984
Award CM 1985
Blooms Pink; medium to large,
double, camellia-shaped,
produced in clusters;
recurrent; light scent
Height and spread 3 × 2 ft (90 × 60 cm)
Other uses Bedding; standards

SEXY REXY has exquisite blooms of high quality which last well in water. They are borne on a bushy plant with glossy green foliage.

STANDARD (TREE) ROSES

Certain roses adapt very well to being grown as standards and make striking features in the garden.

As a stunning specimen plant or as a means of adding height to a bed or border, few plants can better a standard rose in full flower. The important point to remember when growing standard roses is that their impact is lost if they are planted among rampant bush varieties. They look much better rising above low ground-cover roses or flowerbeds.

Choose a standard suitable for your site. For example, some of the short-growing standards, particularly the smaller ground-cover roses and patio varieties, give an extra dimension to small gardens and patios. On a larger scale, a solitary weeping standard surrounded by lawn is a magnificent sight when in full bloom.

Most roses available from nurseries and garden centers are propagated on a rootstock at soil level. However, in the case of standards the rootstock is grown to produce a tall stem, also referred to as a cane. The head of a standard rose can be budded on stems of differing heights, the length of stem defining the type of standard. Thus a half-standard is 1½–2 ft (45–60 cm); a full standard 3–3½ ft (90 cm–1.1 m); a shrub standard 3½–4 ft (1.1–1.2 m); and a weeping, or umbrella, standard 4½ ft (1.4 m). Iron or wire "umbrellas" are sold to train weeping standards. However, these frames should not be necessary if a truly weeping variety is used.

In theory, any rose variety can be grown as a standard, but in practice this is not always so. For reasons unknown, most older varieties produce unsatisfactory results, and some are completely incompatible with a standard stem. However, modern varieties give good results. Patio and ground-cover roses are ideal as half-standards. Bushy Floribundas and Hybrid Teas, the more vigorous ground-cover roses and lax shrubs work well as full standards and shrub standards. Some of the big, very lax ramblers make admirable weeping standards. The vigorous, upright varieties, however, look incongruous grown in this way.

Standard roses must be grown in sheltered positions as they will not tolerate wind. Their shallow root systems make them vulnerable to wind rock; if buffeted about, a standard will never do well. Wherever they are planted, standards must be well staked. Use either a hardwood stake of heavy straight-grained lumber, which has been treated with a non-toxic wood preservative; or a metal post. Attach the stem of the rose firmly to the stake or post with at least two tree ties or strips of well-secured webbing (the number of ties will depend on the height of the stem).

This white standard rose adds a further touch of elegance to the clipped box and soft colors of a formal potager garden.

DOROTHY PERKINS (RAMBLER)

Parentage	R. wichuraiana × Madame Gabriel Luizet
Breeder	Jackson and Perkins 1901
Blooms	Rose pink; small, double, produced in dense clusters; summer-flowering; very little scent
Height and spread	12 × 10 ft (3.7 × 3 m)
Other uses	Fences; trees; pergolas

DOROTHY PERKINS is the rose to choose to make a weeping standard, or "umbrella," of spectacular proportions. It is a rampant rambler with the vigor to cover a vast area. Plant it in an open position to make the most of its fantastic display of flowers and shiny green foliage. It may need protection against mildew.

EXCELSA (RAMBLER)

Synonym	Red Dorothy Perkins
Breeder	Walsh 1909
Blooms	Crimson; small, double, produced in dense clusters; recurrent; little scent
Height and spread	12 × 10 ft (3.7 × 3 m)
Other uses	Trees; arches; pergolas

EXCELSA makes a magnificent weeping standard. It is, by nature, a rampant rambler and produces long trailing stems studded with flowers. It has small leaves. Mildew may be a problem in autumn.

KENT (GROUND COVER)

Synonym	Poulcov; Pyrenees; White Cover
Breeder	Poulsen 1990
Awards	PIT 1990; CM Glasgow 1992
Blooms	Pure white; small, double, produced in clusters; recurrent; scent
Height and spread	1½ × 2½ ft (45 × 75 cm)
Other uses	Patios; confined spaces

KENT is a small-flowered, free-flowering rose with a short, bushy habit and dark green foliage. It was one of the first ground-cover roses to gain recognition in international trials. It makes an excellent half-standard and is perfect for a small space.

MATANGI (FLORIBUNDA)

Synonym	Macman
Parentage	Seedling × Picasso
Breeder	McGredy 1974
Award	PIT 1974
Blooms	Rich orange red with a white eye and a pale silver reverse; large, double, produced in small clusters; recurrent; scent
Height and spread	3 × 2 ft (90 × 60 cm)
Other uses	Beds

MATANGI excels as a standard with its bushy growth and dark, glossy foliage. However, the most outstanding feature of this cluster-flowered bush rose is its delicately shaded flowers, aptly described as "hand-painted," This is the most successful of the hand-painted roses, showing resistance to disease and standing up well to wet weather.

THE WILD ROSE GARDEN

Free-growing wild rose shrubs have great charm and attract wildlife into the garden.

The wild, or species, roses are the forerunners of our modern varieties. They have dainty foliage, delicate flowers and bright hips, although, unlike most modern cultivars, they have only a single flush of flowers in summer. In the case of *R. xanthina* "Canary Bird," for example, this can be outstanding (see page 151). Most wild roses are hardy, but they vary greatly in height: from 6 in (15 cm) to enormous specimens reaching 40 ft (12 m).

The best place for growing wild roses is in a wild garden. Planted singly, or in groups of three, they look dramatic in flower and provide cover for wildlife throughout the year. Some, such as *R. glauca* (see page 151) with its attractive purplish foliage, look good planted in a border. Others, such as *R. moyesii* "Geranium" (see page 149), add to the hues of autumn with a spectacular show of hips.

The most important fact to remember when growing wild roses is that they will not tolerate being cut back or pruned. The only exception is removing dead wood. In this case a complete branch should be cut out as close as possible to the ground using a pruning saw.

Wild roses tolerate a wide range of soils, although they favor slightly acid conditions. Like all roses, they prefer full sun and require good drainage. Before planting dig over the soil and incorporate plenty of organic material, such as well-rotted manure. This will encourage the plants to start growing quickly. Make sure the area around the base is kept clear of grass and weeds, and apply a mulch in spring when the ground is thoroughly moist. Wild roses benefit from regular feeding and, although they may be troubled by aphids, they rarely suffer from black spot or mildew.

Many wild roses produce great quantities of hips which are very beautiful and a great feast for the birds in the autumn. Rosa pomifera duplex has large round hips reminiscent of small apples.

ROSA HUGONIS (SPECIES)

Synonyms   Father Hugo's rose; golden
rose of China

Origin   Introduced from China in
1899

Blooms   Primrose yellow; small,
single; summer-flowering;
scent

Height and spread   8 × 6 ft (2.4 × 1.8 m)

Other uses   Borders; bush

ROSA HUGONIS has graceful, arching stems which
will eventually form a large, almost thornless
plant. The dainty fern-like foliage is gray green
and an asset to any garden. This is one of the
earliest roses to flower.

ROSA MACROPHYLLA (SPECIES)

Origin   Introduced from the
Himalayas in 1818

Blooms   Cerise; large, single; summer-
flowering; scent

Height and spread   10 × 4 ft (3 × 1.2 m)

Other uses   Bush

ROSA MACROPHYLLA has a vigorous, upright habit.
The leaves are large, purplish green and finely
divided. The hips are the outstanding feature of
this fine rose. They are orange-red and very
large, and hang on the plant like small pears.

ROSA MOYESII GERANIUM (SPECIES)

Synonym   R. Geranium

Origin   R. *moyesii* seedling, selected
in 1938

Blooms   Orange red with creamy
stamens; small, single;
summer-flowering; scent

Height and spread   6 × 4 ft (1.8 × 1.2 m)

Other uses   Bush

ROSA MOYESII GERANIUM is a spectacular plant for
the smaller garden. Its neat arching growth is
covered with light green foliage. The flowers
are beautiful and the flask-shaped orange-red
hips hang in profusion in the autumn.

ROSA PIMPINELLIFOLIA (SPECIES)

Synonyms   R. *spinosissima*; burnet rose,
Scotch briar

Origin   Introduced before 1600

Blooms   White, pink, red, purple or
yellow; generally small,
rounded, single or double;
summer-flowering; light scent

Height and spread   7 × 5 ft (2 × 1.5 m)

Other uses   Borders; bush; cut flowers

ROSA PIMPINELLIFOLIA makes a dense, spreading
and thorny plant with small leaves. The flowers
are followed by masses of small black hips.
This is an extremely variable species and is
frequently classified as a group. In many cases
the different forms and variants have been
named. For instance, the bright yellow-flowered
form, the yellow rose of Texas, is also known as
R. × harisonni. These roses were extremely
popular in the 1800s.

R O S A   R O X B U R G H I I *(S P E C I E S)*

Synonyms	Burr rose; chestnut rose; chinquapin rose
Origin	Introduced from China in 1824
Blooms	Lilac pink; medium, single; summer-flowering; sweet scent
Height and spread	6 × 4 ft (1.8 × 1.2 m)
Other uses	Bush

ROSA ROXBURGHII is grown primarily for its large green hips. These are covered in spines and resemble thistle heads. The stiff stems are also very prickly. An attractive feature is the tawny brown bark, which flakes with age. This spreading rose makes a curious but interesting plant of architectural merit.

R O S A   S E R I C E A   P T E R A C A N T H A *(S P E C I E S)*

Synonyms	R. omeiensis pteracantha; R. sericea subsp. omeiensis forma pteracantha; winged thorn rose
Origin	Introduced from China in 1890
Blooms	White, small, single, only four petals; summer-flowering; no scent
Height and spread	10 × 6 ft (3 × 1.8 m)
Other uses	Bush

ROSA SERICEA PTERACANTHA is grown mainly for the huge wedge-shaped thorns which appear on its young wood. The thorns are ruby-red and appear translucent when seen against the morning or evening light. Prune this rose regularly to encourage new growth bearing colorful thorns. It is a vigorous rose with light green, fern-like foliage.

R O S A   E L E G A N T U L A   P E R S E T O S A *(S P E C I E S)*

Synonyms	R. farreri var. persetosa; threepenny-bit rose
Origin	Introduced from China in 1914
Blooms	Lilac pink; very small, single; summer-flowering; light scent
Height and spread	6 × 4 ft (1.8 × 1.2 m)
Other uses	Bush

ROSA ELEGANTULA PERSETOSA has the smallest flowers in the genus *Rosa*, which accounts for the name threepenny-bit rose. It has wiry, upright stems and small leaves. In autumn the flowers are followed by minute red hips.

R O S A   S W E G I N Z O W I I *(S P E C I E S)*

Origin	Introduced from China in 1910
Blooms	Bright pink; large, single; summer-flowering
Height and spread	10 × 6 ft (3 × 1.8 m)
Other uses	Bush

ROSA SWEGINZOWII has an elegant upright habit and fern-like foliage. However, the stems are armed with vicious thorns of various sizes. In autumn the great number of bright red, flask-shaped hips makes a spectacular display.

ROSA XANTHINA CANARY BIRD (SPECIES)

Synonym R. xanthina spontanea

Origin Intoduced from China in 1907

Blooms Bright yellow; small, single; spring-flowering; sweet scent

Height and spread 8 × 6 ft (2.4 × 1.8 m)

Other uses Hedges; bush; standards

ROSA XANTHINA CANARY BIRD forms a neat shrub with dainty fern-like foliage. The whole plant is smothered with flowers in late spring. It requires little maintenance apart from occasional thinning out to remove very old wood. On acid soils there may be some dieback, but new growth will soon develop. This is probably the most widely grown of the species roses.

ROSA EGLANTERIA (SPECIES)

Synonyms R. rubiginosa; eglantine rose; sweet briar

Origin A native of Europe and South-west Asia

Blooms Pink, medium-sized, single, cup-shaped; summer-flowering; sweet scent

Height and spread 10 × 6 ft (3 × 1.8 m)

Other uses Bush

ROSA EGLANTERIA has a wonderful fragrance. Even the young growth, when bruised, exudes a powerful sweet perfume. It is a robust, vigorous plant with an arching habit. The flowers are followed by a harvest of red hips. These turn black with age.

COMPLICATA (SPECIES)

Synonym R. gallica var. complicata

Origin Ancient

Blooms Bright pink; large, single; summer-flowering; scent

Height and spread 12 × 12 ft (3.7 × 3.7 m)

Other uses Hedges; trees; bush

COMPLICATA, given space, will develop into a very large, semi-rambling clump, providing plenty of cover for wildlife. In mid-summer, when it is in full flower, it looks magnificent. The foliage is an attractive grayish green, but beware of the stems as they are very thorny.

ROSA GLAUCA (SPECIES)

Synonym R. rubrifolia

Origin Introduced in the early 1800s

Blooms Deep pink; small, single; summer-flowering; little scent

Height and spread 10 × 6 ft (3 × 1.8 m)

Other uses Bush

ROSA GLAUCA is a favorite plant of garden designers who admire its grayish-purple foliage and arching violet-purple stems, tinged with red in autumn. It is almost thornless and a vigorous grower. The dainty flowers are followed in autumn by large quantities of bright red hips.

ROSA HIGHDOWNENIS (SPECIES)

Synonym	R. × highdownensis
Origin	R. moyesii seedling
Breeder	Stern 1928
Blooms	Deep pink; small to medium-sized, single; summer-flowering; moderate scent
Height and spread	9 × 4 ft (2.7 × 1.2 m)
Other uses	Specimen

HIGHDOWNENSIS bears enormous flask-shaped, orange-red hips in autumn. It is a vigorous rose with open, arching growth and coppery-colored foliage. The thorns are large and sharp.

ROSA VILLOSA (SPECIES)

Synonyms	R. pomifera; apple rose
Origin	Introduced from central Europe in about 1761
Blooms	Clear pink; medium, semi-double; summer-flowering; good scent
Height and spread	8 × 5 ft (2.4 × 1.5 m)
Other uses	Borders

ROSA VILLOSA makes a large shrubby plant with long, arching stems and pale, grayish-green foliage. The flowers are borne in small clusters or singly and the petals have an attractive crumpled appearance. However, the chief merit of this variety is the profusion of large, round hips which persist well into winter. These are covered with bristles and at first are orange, but later turn dark purple.

ROSA CANTABRIGIENSIS (SHRUB)

Synonym	R. × cantabrigiensis
Parentage	Probably R. hugonis × R. sericea
Breeder	Cambridge Botanic Garden 1931
Blooms	Primrose yellow; small, single; summer flowering; scent
Height and spread	12 × 8 ft (3.7 × 2.4 m)
Other uses	Borders

CANTABRIGIENSIS is a very early-flowering variety with delightful fern-like foliage. The flowers are larger than its R. hugonis parent and are borne on long stems made the previous summer, so take care not to prune them out. This rose grows vigorously and, provided it has adequate space, will eventually form a magnificent specimen. Small, round, orange hips develop by the end of summer to give interest late in the year.

ROSA SOULIEANA (SPECIES)

Origin	Introduced from China in 1896
Blooms	White; small, single, produced in clusters; summer-flowering; scent
Height and spread	8 × 8 ft (2.4 × 2.4 m)
Other uses	Landscaping

ROSA SOULIEANA is outstanding for its foliage. This is composed of small leaves which are gray-green, almost silvery in appearance. The arching stems are also grayish in color and form a bushy plant which requires little in the way of pruning. In autumn it is smothered with trusses of small, orange-red hips.

ROSA WOODSII (SPECIES)

Synonym	R. woodsii var. fendleri
Origin	Introduced from North America in 1888
Blooms	Bright lilac-pink; small, single; summering flowering; scent
Height and spread	6 × 5 ft (1.8 × 1.5 m)
Other uses	Borders

ROSA WOODSII forms a graceful shrub of upright habit. Its gray-green stems are well furnished with grayish foliage. The flowers are borne on thin, pliable stems formed the previous year. In autumn small, pear-shaped hips become bright red and last well into winter.

ROSA FORRESTIANA (SPECIES)

Origin	Introduced from western China in 1918
Blooms	Pinkish crimson; semi-double, small; summer flowering; slight scent
Height and spread	10 × 8 ft (3 × 2.4 m)
Other uses	Borders

ROSA FORRESTIANA eventually makes a large plant densely covered with purplish green foliage. The flowers have a central boss of creamy buff stamens and are quite showy. However, it is the display of red, bottle-shaped hips that really sets this rose apart. The hips are produced in quantity and persist well into the winter.

ROSA HELEN KNIGHT (SPECIES)

Synonym	R. ecae "Helen Knight"
Origin	R. ecae hybrid introduced by Knight 1966
Blooms	Clear yellow; very small, single; summer-flowering; light scent
Height and spread	8 × 4 ft (2.4 × 1.2 m)
Other uses	Semi-climber

HELEN KNIGHT is one of the first roses to flower, carrying its blooms on long stems. It has dainty, fern-like foliage and grows vigorously to develop into a beautiful shrub, provided it is in a warm situation. It does well against a sunny wall and can be trained as a climber.

ROSA MULLIGANII (SPECIES)

Origin	Discovered in Yunnan c.1900
Introduced	Farrer (Wisley) 1919
Blooms	White; small, single, produced in large clusters; summer-flowering; slight scent
Height and spread	15 × 10 ft (4.5 × 3 m)
Other uses	Trees; pergolas

ROSA MULLIGANII is a spectacular plant covered in a mass of white flowers which hang down slightly. It grows quickly and, lightly pruned, can be used as a specimen plant or allowed to climb into trees and over pergolas.

HARDINESS ZONES FOR ROSES

Roses are resilient plants and thrive in temperate climates in hardiness Zones 4 to 9.

The majority of garden roses tolerate considerable levels of frost, surviving temperatures as low as -2° C (14° F). However, if temperatures persist below this for any length of time protection in the form of mulching and wrapping is required. Roses are generally assumed to be cold-hardy in Zones 4 to 9, with protection. Plant catalogs usually do not include hardiness zones for roses, because success with the plants depends on other factors besides temperature, and because winter protection can help a rose bush survive very cold weather.

The limits of the average annual minimum temperatures for each zone

	Zone 1	Below -50° F (-10° C)
	Zone 2	-40 to -50° F (-9 to -10° C)
	Zone 3	-30 to -40° F (-8 to -9° C)
	Zone 4	-20 to -30° F (-6 to -8° C)
	Zone 5	-10 to -20° F (-5 to -6° C)
	Zone 6	0 to -10° F (-4 to -5° C)
	Zone 7	10 to 0° F (-3 to -4° C)
	Zone 8	20 to 10° F (-1 to -3° C)
	Zone 9	30 to 20° F (0 to -1° C)
	Zone 10	40 to 30° F (1 to 0° C)

Temperatures in the rose-growing regions of the Southern Hemisphere and Northern Europe do not have to contend with these problems, fortunately. However, it is worth noting that the majority of winter fatalities in these areas are because the plants become waterlogged (with roots in badly drained soil that is permanently wet), rather than by very low temperatures alone.

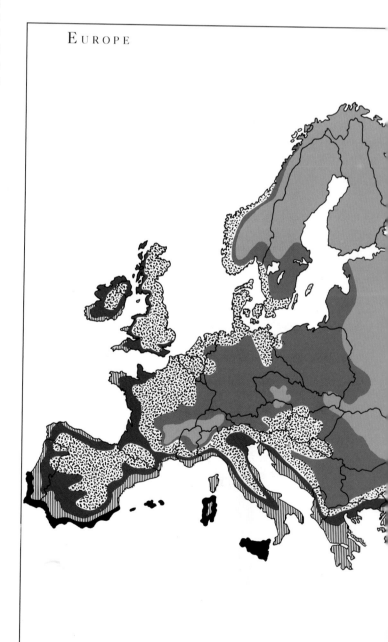

EUROPE

AUSTRALIA AND NEW ZEALAND

SOUTH AFRICA

NORTH AMERICA

USEFUL ADDRESSES

ROSE SOCIETIES

There are many specialist organizations whose primary object is to encourage and spread knowledge of the rose. Many hold large rose shows, publish annual and quarterly magazines, produce much valuable information on rose cultivation and sponsor frequent lectures.

This is a selection of the principal rose societies who are all members of the World Federation of Rose Societies.

Argentina
Rose Society of Argentina
Libertador 408 16B
1001 Buenos Aires

Australia
National Rose Society of Australia
271b Balmore Road
North Balwyn
Victoria 3104

Canada
Canadian Rose Society
110 Fairfax Crescent
Scarborough
Ontario M1L 1Z8

France
Société Française des Roses
6 Rue J B Couty
69009 Lyon

Germany
Verein Deutscher Rosenfreunde
Waldseestrasse 14
D-76530 Baden-Baden

Great Britain
The Royal National Rose Society
Chiswell Green
St Albans
Hertfordshire AL2 3NR

Italy
Associazione Italiana della Rosa
Roseta Niso Fumagalli
Villa Reale
20052 Monza (MI)

Japan
Japan Rose Society
3-9-5 Oyamdai
Setagaya-ku
Tokyo
158 Japan

The Netherlands
Nederlandse Rozenvereniging
Cromhoutstraat 36
6971 AV Brummen

New Zealand
National Rose Society of New Zealand
PO Box 66
Bunnythorpe
Palmerston North

Northern Ireland
Rose Society of Northern Ireland
10 Eastleigh Drive
Belfast BT4 3DX

Norway
Norwegian Rose Society
Smiuvn 8
N-0982 Oslo

Pakistan
Pakistan National Rose Society
36 Nazimddin Road, F-7/1
Islamabad

South Africa
Federation of Rose Societies of South Africa
Box 95738
Waterkloof
0145 RSA

Spain
Asociacion Espanola de la Rose
Rosaleda Ramon Ortiz
Parque del Oeste
28008 Madrid

USA
American Rose Society
PO Box 30,000
Shreveport
Louisiana 71130-0030

ROSE GARDENS

There are very few countries with a temperate climate that do not have at least one large garden where roses are well grown and, of equal importance, correctly labeled. Information and advice is readily given to visitors, and many owners are only too pleased to discuss varieties and compare notes.

This is a selection of gardens around the world famed for their roses and well worth a visit during the flowering season.

Great Britain and Northern Ireland

The Gardens of the Rose
The Royal National Rose Society
Chiswell Green
St. Albans
Hertfordshire
A national collection of all types of rose beautifully displayed. The famous rose trial for new introductions also takes place on this site.

RHS Garden
Wisley
Nr. Woking
Surrey
This 240-acre garden of the Royal Horticultural Society includes many superbly grown shrub and climbing roses. There is also a fine collection of the newest introductions.

RHS Garden
Rosemoor
Torrington
Devon
A famous garden given to the Royal Horticultural Society in 1988 which displays a wide variety of roses.

Queen Mary's Garden
Inner Circle
Regent's Park
London
Here, in the centre of London, can be found the famous Rose Garden with its wide selection of old and modern roses.

Sir Thomas and Lady Dixon Park
Belfast
Northern Ireland
A recently reconstructed rose garden, with a well-displayed historical section and modern rose trials.

Eire

St. Anne's Park
Dublin
This includes large beds of superbly grown modern roses and a unique miniature rose garden.

France

Roserie du Parc de Bagatelle
Paris
Pergolas and arches dominate this garden in the center of Paris, together with its famous trials.

Germany

Sangerhausen Rosarium
Sangerhausen
This is reputed to have the largest collection of roses, old and new, in the world.

Zweibruken City Rose Garden
Zweibruken
An interesting and wide-ranging collection of roses old and new, displayed in asssociation with herbaceous plants and modern architecture.

The Netherlands

Westbrook Park
The Hague
The site of the most famous rose trials in Europe, set out in a beautiful garden with all the modern varieties.

USA

American Rose Center
Shreveport
Louisiana
A new garden built and planted with imagination and style.

Huntingdon Botanical Gardens
San Marino
California
An extensive collection of old garden roses and the home of a famous library.

Canada

Centennial Rose Garden
Burlington
Ontario
A large collection of modern and historical roses.

Australia

Royal Botanic Gardens
South Yarra
Victoria
An extensive collection of the old and the new.

I N D E X

CREDITS

Quarto would like to thank the following for kindly
providing pictures used in this book.

Key: *a* above, *b* below, *c* center, *l* left, *r* right

Pat Brindley 13, 80*bc*, 136*a*, 137*a*, 148; **Alan L. Detrick** 23*a*, 137*bc*; **Dickson
Nurseries Ltd** 15, 101*bc*; **Garden Matters** 25, 82, 86; **Garden Picture Library**
31 (Jerry Pavia); **Peter A. Haring** 5*r*, 83*a*, 84*ac*, 90*bc*, 92*b*, 95*ac*, *bc* & *b*, 103*b*, 110*a*,
113*a*, 114*ac*, 115*ac*, 117*ac*, 118*ac*, 121*ac*, 125*b*, 127*bc*, 133*ac*, 135*bc*, 151*a*; **Harkness**
69*a*, 91*b*, 136*bc*, 137*ac*; **Image Bank** 142, 143; **Paul E. Jerabek** 118*b*, 149*a*;
Mike Lowe 8*b*, 62*a*, 67*a* & *ac* (Brenda Louches), 85*b*, 87*bc*, 92*bc*, 103*a*, 110*bc*,
116*b*, 117*a*, 119*bc*, 129*bc*, 133*a*, 135*ac*, 147*bc*, 149*b*, 152*ac*; **John Mattock** 51, 67*bc*
& *b*, 72*a* & *bc*, 73*b*, 77*a*, 80*b*, 84*ac*, 87*a*, 87*bc*, 89*ac*, *bc* & *b*, 92*a*, 93*b*, 96*bc* , 97*b*,
100*ac*, 101*ac*, 107*a* & *b*, 109*b*, 110*b*, 111*bc* & *b*, 113*ac*, *bc* & *b*, 114*a* & *b*, 116*bc*, 119*a*
& *ac*, 122*b*, 123*ac*, 128*ac* & *b*, 131*ac* & *bc*, 133*bc*, 135*b*, 145*a* & *bc*, 150*ac*, 152*bc* & *b*;
Clive Nichols 2-3, 7, 139, 140, 146; **Photo/Nats** 8*a* (Virginia Twinam-Smith),
44*a* (Virginia Twinam-Smith), 97*a* (Virginia Twinam-Smith), 103*ac* (Virginia Twinam-Smith), 110*ac* (Ann
Reilly), 121*b* (Albert Squillace), 133*b* (Ann Reilly), 147*a* (Ann Reilly), 153*a* (Jeff
March); **Photos Horticultural** 12, 45, 46, 48-9, 52, 57, 59, 62*b*, 71, 126*a*; **Royal
National Rose Society** 132*bc*; **Harry Smith Horticultural Collection** 9, 14, 17,
21, 22-3, 29, 30, 33, 36, 37, 38, 42-3, 43*r*; 56, 60*l* & *r*; 61, 63, 66, 68*a* & *bc*, 69*ac*, *bc*
& *b*, 70, 73*a* & *bc*, 74, 76*a* & *ac*, 79, 80*a* & *ac*, 81*a*, *ac*, *bc* & *b*, 83*bc* & *b*, 84*a*, 85*a*,
87*ac*, 89*a*, 90, 93*bc*, 94, 95*a*, 96*a*, 97*ac* & *bc*, 98, 99*b*, 101*a* & *b*, 102*ac* & *bc*, 128*a*,
119*b*, 103*bc*, 104, 105*bc*, 107*ac*, 109*a* & *ac*, 112, 116*a*, 117*b*, 119*b*, 120, 128*a*, 130,
131*a*, 132*a* & *ac*, 134, 136*b*, 137*b*, 138, 144*ac* & *bc*, 147*ac* & *b*, 150*bc*, 151*ac* & *b*,
153*ac*, *bc* & *b*; **Peter Stiles** 72*ac*, 77*bc*, 83*ac*, 84*bc*, 85*bc* (Val Foster), 88*ac*, 108*bc*,
109*bc*, 151*bc*; **Carl Wallace** 5*l*; **Warner's Roses** 88*bc* & *b*.

All other photographs are by Ian Howes and are the copyright of
Quarto Publishing.

Whilst every effort has been made to acknowledge copyright-holders, Quarto
would like to apologize should any omissions have been made.